Animal Medicine

"The animal kingdom, in its love and compassion to humans, is always willing to gift us with what we need the most when our souls are in need of teachings, guidance, and medicine. We, however, have lost so much of our connections to the ancient wisdom and the shamanic practices, making it quite difficult to translate the meaning of what is being transmitted. In *Animal Medicine,* the great curandera Erika Buenaflor has gifted us with her deep understanding of ancient shamanism and how we can rescue our sacred relationship with animals, temples, rituals, and ageless wisdom. This book is filled with teachings and practices from a rich culture, kept sacred by the curanderx of Mesoamerica. *Animal Medicine* is here to inspire us to discover and develop our own spiritual path, a path leading to the healing of our body, mind, and soul. Muchas gracias, Erika Buenaflor, for your curandera's gifts to us all."

VERA LOPEZ, COAUTHOR OF *SHAMANIC MYSTERIES OF PERU*

"As a bruja, I want to thank Erika Buenaflor from the bottom of my heart for all the research, love, and dedication she put into this book. *Animal Medicine* is profound, groundbreaking, and perfect for students of all levels! I am fortunate to have experienced Erika's magic in person. She is a loving and strong spirit, a conduit from times past, and her work is here to heal our future generations. I am so elated to give this book five stars for all the valuable secrets Erika shares with us. She is one of the most unique and approachable voices in the shamanic community."

VALERIA RUELAS, THE MEXICAN WITCH AND
AUTHOR OF *COSMOPOLITAN LOVE POTIONS*

"Filled with information and experiential exercises to give you a first-person perspective, this book is a delightful deep dive into Mesoamerican shamanic wisdom! Buenaflor's work is not only valuable for exploring animal spirits from the curanderx perspective but will also augment the relationships with spirits you have already encountered on your shamanic path."

EVELYN C. RYSDYK, AUTHOR OF *SPIRIT WALKING, THE NORSE SHAMAN,*
AND *THE NEPALESE SHAMANIC PATH* (WITH BHOLA BANSTOLA)

"Erika Buenaflor has added significantly to our understanding of curanderismo with her three previous books dealing with cleansing rituals, soul retrieval, and sacred energy. Her new book, *Animal Medicine,* adds to an ever-expanding examination of curanderismo and shamanism, which cannot be complete without understanding the role that animal spirits play in the esoteric and mystical world of human experience."

ANTONIO NOÉ ZAVALETA, PH.D., AUTHOR OF
CURANDERO: HISPANIC ETHNO-PSYCHOTHERAPY & CURANDERISMO

"With *Animal Medicine,* Erika Buenaflor lays an offering at our feet of how to commune with nature and access our animal guides. This comprehensive text is a must-read for anyone looking to connect with ancient Mesoamerican traditions that help us understand our physical world, dreams, animal meanings, myth, and symbolic discourse."

ANGÉLICA M. YAÑEZ, PH.D., EDITOR OF
UNITED STATES HISTORY FROM A CHICANO PERSPECTIVE

"Erika Buenaflor has both researched and had in-depth experience to gather an incredible wealth of wisdom teachings on animal medicine to assist journeyers in their deep connection with animal spirits and allies. If you have a desire to understand how to work with animal medicine, this is definitely the book for you! The imagery is provocative and stirring to the psyche, opening the consciousness to the inner journey."

LINDA STAR WOLF, PH.D., CREATOR OF
VENUS RISING AND SHAMANIC BREATHWORK JOURNEYS
AND AUTHOR OF *SHAMANIC BREATHWORK*

Animal Medicine is a very heartfelt and authentically researched addition to the kingdoms of animal spirit literature and wisdom. Long live Itzamna!"

JAMES ENDREDY, AUTHOR OF *ADVANCED SHAMANISM*
AND *SHAMANIC ALCHEMY*

Animal Medicine

A Curanderismo Guide to Shapeshifting, Journeying, and Connecting with Animal Allies

Erika Buenaflor, M.A., J.D.

Bear & Company
Rochester, Vermont

Bear & Company
One Park Street
Rochester, Vermont 05767
www.BearandCompanyBooks.com

Text stock is SFI certified

Bear & Company is a division of Inner Traditions International

Cataloging-in-Publication Data for this title is available from the Library of Congress

ISBN 978-1-59143-411-5 (print)
ISBN 978-1-59143-412-2 (ebook)

Printed and bound in the United States by Lake Book Manufacturing, Inc. The text stock is SFI certified. The Sustainable Forestry Initiative® program promotes sustainable forest management.

10 9 8 7 6 5 4 3 2 1

Text design and layout by Virginia Scott Bowman
This book was typeset in Garamond Premier Pro and Futura with Kapra Neue used as the display typeface
Black and white animal drawings by Carolina Gutierrez

To send correspondence to the author of this book, mail a first-class letter to the author c/o Inner Traditions • Bear & Company, One Park Street, Rochester, VT 05767, and we will forward the communication, or contact the author directly at **www.realizeyourbliss.com**.

Contents

PART TWO

Animal Allies A to Z

Ancient Mesoamerican Animal Mythologies, Spiritual and Shapeshifting Medicine, and Symbolism

Introduction to Ancient Mesoamerican and Curanderismo Animal Symbolism

The people of ancient Mesoamerica largely understood the fauna around them to be related to and manifestations of the sacred and the cosmos. Animals were thought to serve as messengers or agents for deities or other supernatural beings, connected people with a particular deity or sacred phenomenon, and provided omens. Lay people, fisherman, hunters, and farmers engaged in ritual animal invocations to ensure success in hunting and fishing, prevent animals from doing damage to their fields, and deter ants from certain areas and actions.[1] Diviners, shamans, and healers interpreted the appearance and actions of animals in the physical world and in dreams to assess and determine numerous kinds of everyday situations.[2]

Animals were also prominent in the peoples' myths and legends and served as models and metaphors for their social and natural worlds and symbolic discourse. In addition, they could be found in emblem glyphs of dynasties and may have served as designated guides that were transmitted from one ruler to another within the same dynastic line.[3] Animals were also associated with astrological constellations in codices, stelae, and other cultural platforms and comprised many of the day

1

signs* within their divinatory (260 days) calendar. The innate gifts and powers that animals were understood to embody, represent, and provide access to made them critical actors in the political, religious, and cultural life.

This book will delve into the symbolic discourse and ceremonial rites the ancient Mesoamerican peoples assigned to particular animals and explore the two most common ways we can connect with animals to gain access to their gifts and medicine. The first way is to develop a relationship with them in the physical and spiritual/dream realms and cultivate a symbolic method of communication with them. The second way is through shapeshifting, and this definitely encompasses the physical shapeshifting we see in popular horror movies.

In Mesoamerican *curanderismo* and shamanic traditions there are many ways to shapeshift into an animal, including etheric, astral, joining, bilocation, and physical shapeshifting. Etheric shapeshifting typically involves shifting into an animal through the subtle bodies—the etheric, the emotional, and the mental—that are closest to the physical body. Astral shapeshifting involves shifting through our astral body and is often identified as having an out-of-body experience, or OBE. Joining commonly involves projecting our consciousness into an animal, and bilocation occurs when a person's animating soul energy splits, with one half shifting into an animal form (or some other form) and the other half remaining in the physical body. Physical shapeshifting is when the physical body transforms into an animal.

Despite the rather ubiquitous and diverse traditions of animal shapeshifting in ancient Mesoamerica, popular books on the subject are either unaware of or simply ignore these rich traditions despite the fact that contemporary ethnographies report that they still exist in indigenous towns throughout Mexico and Guatemala. On the academic front,

---

*Day signs were symbolic characters—animals, elements, or sacred items, whose meaning and expressions could be nuanced by a myriad of factors, as explained further in chapter 1. They were also likely understood as animate beings in their own right. (Thompson, *Maya Hieroglyphic Writing*, 69)

while some of these practices were recorded by early sixteenth and seventeenth ethnographers, the analysis of them is sometimes guided by limited understanding of shapeshifting practices or dichotomizing tendencies that link particular practices with either nonmalicious or malicious practices without exploring their complex multivalent symbolism. Modern analysis also often ignores the possibility that these rites were understood as or operated in quantum fields, where many things can be happening at one time, especially if the practitioner has a high degree of mastery over their animating soul energies.

The complex development of mythological symbolic discourse concerning animals was polysemic, multilayered, ambiguous, and idiosyncratic. On one level it was imparted and on another, it was appropriated in a dialectical process whereby it became a subjective reality for the person who was utilizing, reciting, and often generating new meanings and expressions.

In the following chapters, I will compare and contrast various sources, including textual, illustrative, sculptural, and architectural authorities; burial sites and tombs and the sacred items found in these places; pre- and postcontact codices; and sixteenth-, seventeenth-, and eighteenth-century ethnohistorical records. When available, I will identify the geographical and time-bound origins of the sources, including their particular symbolic use of animals in certain rituals.

The codices of ancient Mesoamerica were objects that could enhance the vision of ritual practitioners and provide a more nuanced understanding of the myths often being performed in ritual through the illustrated costuming, colors, body postures, ritual instruments, iconography, and period of the day, and possibly even aid the shaman to foresee the future.[4] I will examine these rituals not simply as practices whose symbolic meanings must be uncovered but rather, as ritual theoretician Catherine Bell encouraged, as actions that generate meanings in the specific context of other sets of meaningful actions and discourses.[5]

While I may separate and identify the geographical and time-bound origins of the symbolic discourse of the ancient Central Mexicans and the Maya in my descriptions, it is important to understand that this does not imply that the creation or exclusive possession of the discourse is limited to that region or period. As Mesoamerican scholar Alfredo López Austin asserts, "Common history and the particular histories of each Mesoamerican culture function[ed] dialectically to form a Mesoamerican vision rich in regional and local expression."[6]

Ancient Mesoamerican people shared basic concepts about the human body and human life, a basic deity pantheon, principal iconographic symbols, and a core complex of mythical beliefs. As Mesoamerican scholar Oswaldo Chinchilla Mazariegos points out, "Mesoamerican myths are better understood as derived from a common core of ancient beliefs that diverged in multiple regional variants."[7]

There are oftentimes mythological themes and meanings related to animals that are resilient and can be traced throughout many regions, cultures, and periods of ancient Mesoamerica.[8] One likely reason for this is that the sacred gifts and meanings that animals were associated with typically reflected their physical attributes and natural habits and instincts. These included their methods for hunting/gathering food, mating, and grooming themselves as well as where they resided and ventured, how they moved, and whether they were nocturnal or diurnal.[9]

In ancient Mesoamerican mythologies, narrative and illustrative, animals were involved in the creation of the world—how it was made or discovered, how elements in nature were created, and how races or tribes originated and acquired maize and other foods.[10] These mythologies also often explained how animals obtained various characteristics and propensities, and they communicated themes and meanings with regard to a particular animal's sacred qualities, actions, deeds, and associations.

To ascertain this symbolic discourse, I will look at the shamanic interpretation of dreams and the appearance of animals in them, as well as the ritual use of animal-related medicinal and magical remedies. The uses of animals in cures were quite numerous, even more so than those of plants. Animals' magical curing abilities were typically tied to their physical and behavioral characteristics and the myths they were associated with.[11] The flexibility of small snakes and the many movable joints of centipedes, for example, were utilized in remedies to alleviate stiffness. The speed and dexterity of hares and rabbits made them good candidates for ailing extremities.[12] There were also numerous invocations made to animals to plead for their help in banishing an illness from the body of the patient, and particular animals were sometimes considered both the omen and the cause of illness and were identified in these invocations as metaphors of the illness.[13]

When I am unfamiliar with the specific term the ancient Mesoamericans used to identify a practitioner, I use the term *curanderx** to describe individuals among the precontact and colonial Mexica and Maya, who connected with animal medicine by creating or facilitating magical and medicinal animal concoctions, engaging in animal shapeshifting, or interpreting dreams, omens related to animals, or the meanings of their codices or the day signs of their calendars. I am not opposed to the use of the term *shaman* for these practitioners. I have used this term when I was unaware of the indigenous name of the practitioner's specialty.

The term *witchcraft* rather than *shamanism* is typically used when describing the apparent misdeeds that were being accomplished with magic during shapeshifting practices or the misuse of soul animating energies. This encompasses the trend to identify the actions of the curanderx as witchcraft rather than shamanism, particularly in the interpretation of Classic Maya vase artwork. This imagery often revealed more insidious conduct, such as sending soul illnesses or absconding with soul pieces.

It is important to note that per the ethnographic records a good majority of ancient healing practitioners practiced magic, divination, seeing and journeying into nonordinary realms, and even physical

---

*I continue to follow the trend of progressive Latinx communities that are using *x* in place of *a/o* and *as/os* at the end of gendered words. The use of the *x* is intended to transcend static gender binaries.

shapeshifting, blurring the lines between *brujeria* (witchcraft) and shamanism. As a *curandera,* I routinely practice magic, divination, healing, and trance journeying, and so did my mentors. Consequently, I feel the term *curanderx* is more useful in describing these practitioners as it is more common and accepted that curanderx are skilled in diverse arts that are associated with both shamanism and witchcraft.

I limit the scope of my analysis to the Central Mexican Postclassic peoples and the Maya generally of the Classic and Postclassic periods largely due to my own background and training as a curandera. My four primary mentors were proficient in Yucatec Maya curanderismo traditions, beliefs, and practices. Two of them also associated themselves with Nahua traditions. My Maya mentors, Don Tomas and Don Fernando in particular, shared many stories and teachings concerning curanderx who could shapeshift into animals and their different types of shapeshifting practices. In my early mentorship periods, I had quite a few different types of shapeshifting experiences in my dreams and meditations, and I had a lot of questions for my mentors and conversations with them about animal shapeshifting practices. I recognize that clean lines of continuity between ancient and modern Mesoamerican traditions and beliefs do not exist. Nevertheless, enough of the ancient Mesoamerican worldviews survived over the centuries to permit suggestive analogies.[14] These correlations are offered as suggestions rather than definitive conclusions about animal shapeshifting practices.

This book, like my other books, is intended to be a bridge between the academic and spiritual. I use the term *spiritual* to include nonreligious, pagan, religious, and heart-centered practices—basically any kind of tradition or practice that involves believing in some kind of divine power and the rites that arise or are related to those beliefs. Whether or not we have actual blood ties with ancient Mesoamerican indigenous traditions, some of us resonate with and feel intuitively drawn to this wisdom and apply its sacred essence to our spiritual practices and traditions.

Regardless of where we come from, anyone who is willing to do the diligent research and respects and acknowledges these traditions has the right to share this sacred information. I encourage us to lovingly and consciously decolonize our hearts and minds and focus more on conscious respect and reclamation of these traditions rather than their dogmatic control.

The species of animals covered in this book will primarily encompass the ones that were ubiquitous in the mythology of ancient Mesoamerica to discern the symbolic discourse concerning these animals. With regard to the Maya, because the majority of my research is centered in the Classic and Postclassic periods, the animals studied will predominantly entail those that inhabited the lowland tropical forests, where much of the Classic period unfolded, and the northern Yucatán and southern areas of Guatemala and Belize for the Postclassic period. For the ancient Central Mexican peoples, my research primarily focuses on the Postclassic period, so this will include animals from what is now Oaxaca, Guerrero, Puebla, Veracruz, Tlaxcala, Morelos, Aguascalientes, Queretaro, Hidalgo, Guanajuato, Durango, Zacatecas, San Luis Potosí, Mexico (state), and Mexico City.

The animals examined will include various types of vertebrates (fish, amphibians, reptiles, birds, and mammals) and invertebrates (insects, arachnids, mollusks, and worms). It will also include zoomorphic animals, or mythological animals that combined more than one animal and were often thought to have special powers.[15] There was a general perception among the ancient Mesoamerican peoples that there were ranking orders within the classification of animals and, of course, among the animal kingdom, which was reflected in the mythological symbolic discourse that this book will explore.

ANIMAL SPIRIT GUIDES

Because there are so many terms involved when working with animal medicine, guides, and shapeshifting practices, I use the term *animal spirit guide* to encompass all of the diverse types of sacred relationships in which the animal acts as some kind of spiritual guide or coessence. An animal coessence is an animal with which we share a soul energy signature, typically since birth, and similar primal traits and inclinations.[16] By being born on the same day, we acquire the same animating soul energy as that of an animal or species of animal, and we tend to have a particular affinity for one another. We can also increase our animating soul energy every time we connect with, or simply intend to connect with, our animal coessence. The animating soul energy we gain, of course, correlates with the type of connection we make or attempt to make with them.

It is important to mention that while an animal spirit guide may include an animal coessence, not every animal spirit guide will be a coessence. Generally, people have one animal coessence but can have up to two.

As I discuss in greater detail in *Curanderismo Soul Retrieval*, determining the identity of our animal coessence can be done through divination work, take place in dreams or vision quests, or be determined by a curanderx. Most importantly, our animal coessence will make us aware of its identity when we are ready to receive it and will appear to us three or four times at pivotal points in our lives.

It is possible that in some animal shapeshifting practices or relationships, the animal may not serve as a guide or coessence. If that is the case, then the practices discussed in this book may not be applicable, as they presume, on some level, a genuine and humble understanding that any and all animals can serve as a guide at some point in our lives. However, the animal spiritual connection, symbolism, and communication discussed here go beyond our relationships with an animal coessence and again can include any and all of our sacred relationships with animals.

BREAKDOWN OF THE BOOK

The first chapter in part 1 will discuss the pertinent gifts of the nonordinary realms—the Upperworld, Middleworld, and Underworld—and the animals and particular animal traits that were associated with them. I will then delve into how we can connect with animals and obtain sacred medicine in these nonordinary realms. I will also explore the different ways to induce a trance state and journey into a nonordinary realm and connect with an animal as well as critical keys to understanding the meaning of what we saw in those trance journeys. I will include as well a personal story of the medicine I obtained from the Upperworld by honoring a growing relationship with an Upperworld animal.

The second chapter will examine the three primary animating soul energies that were likely used in various degrees for shapeshifting purposes and explore how to garner them for our own practices. I will also delve into some of the different recorded animal shapeshifting practices of ancient Mesoamerica as well as those traditions my mentors discussed with me or I have personally experienced. In addition, I will describe ways to begin to develop shapeshifting skills and the many benefits of doing so and share how my husband's shapeshifting experience helped to develop his spiritual awareness and release attachment to roles and identities.

The third chapter will explore ways to develop a communication system with an animal we feel some kind of spiritual connection to. It will include cultivating a communication system with animals through familiarizing ourselves with their habits and traits, understanding intuitive energy surges, journaling, developing intuition, and practicing shamanic dreamwork, automatic writing, and rituals. I will also share my client's inspirational story of how she developed her symbolic communication with her animal spirit guide, trusted the message, and realized justice and resolution as a result.

Part 2 will explore the particular ancient Mesoamerican mythologies and ceremonial rites of seventy-six animals that were the most prevalent in their spiritual symbolic discourse. This section will be organized alphabetically and highlight the following information about the animals: the nonordinary realm they were associated with, their spiritual and shapeshifting medicine, and their symbolic meanings should we see them in a dream or trance journey or on the physical plane and feel they have a message for us.

GOALS OF THE BOOK

The principal aims of this book are twofold: (1) to collect and preserve this Mesoamerican indigenous ancient wisdom and provide accessible ways of drawing from it to enrich our lives in positive ways and (2) to extend the analysis of ancient Mesoamerican animal shapeshifting practices beyond the study of physical shapeshifting.

The diverse and fascinating relationships that ancient Mesoamerican peoples had with animals are generally very different from the relationships we tend to have with them in contemporary Western society. To be aware of an animal's characteristics, medicine, messages, and energies, including how our own energies are affected by their presence, we must be present, aware, and mindful. When we engage life by being so, we can begin to experience the diverse richness it has to offer us. This book will explore ways for us to see and ideally experience nature and life in new exciting and ways, connect with animal medicine for guidance and healing, draw on an animal's primal instincts in a healthy and empowering manner, become more in tune with and learn how to work with energies, especially animating soul energies, and much more.

For Latinx and Xicanx peoples, learning and reclaiming our indigenous traditions that have been taken from us by the complex processes of colonization is medicine in and of itself. Cultural reclamation can greatly inspire soul healing, retrieval, and revival. The symbolic discourse and offered methods discussed to develop our own symbolic modes of communication, understanding, and connection with animals are also intended to inspire us to discover, define, and develop our spirituality and spirituality-related practices for ourselves.

To truly decolonize our spiritual practices we need to allow ourselves to create a space to discover what feels right for us and question and be critical of anyone or anything that proscribes what our path should look like and entail. If and when we are called to learn and draw from our indigenous practices, we also need to define for ourselves what feels enlightening, uplifting, empowering, applicable, and relevant to us in our personal life—breathing our own unique sacred essence energies into these beautiful traditions. Regardless of culture, race, ethnicity, and traditions, learning these intuitive and heart-centered earth practices and developing a safe, fun, and exploratory space of creation can heal and revive our spirit on many levels.

I hope this book will also help to expand the study of ancient Mesoamerican animal shapeshifting practices to include the consideration of practices beyond physical shapeshifting along with the divergent ways animating soul energies may have come into play in these practices. For instance, there are many documented indications from seventeenth-century ethnographers that animal shapeshifting included bilocation. Approaching these diverse and dynamic practices with a narrow purview of simply looking at one type of physical shapeshifting practice to determine whether a shapeshifting took place can limit our understanding of these practices and the diverse and fascinating roles and actions the shapeshifters may have been playing.

PART ONE

Connecting to
Animal Spirit Guides

*Historical Background, Meditative
Exercises, and Trance Journeys*

1
Animal Contact and Medicine in the Nonordinary Realms

The ancient Mesoamericans commonly divided the world into two forms: a quadripartite form, which was horizontally organized into four cardinal spaces with a center in the middle, and a tripartite form, which was a vertical division of the nonordinary realms of Underworld, Middleworld, and Upperworld. Each nonordinary realm had its own division and ordering; sacred gifts, insight, challenges, and medicine; and deities, ancestors, supernatural beings, and animals that were associated with it (and sometime other realms as well).

An animal's physical attributes, natural habits and instincts, the time of the day they were most active, and related mythologies determined which nonordinary realm(s) they would have passage to and dominion over. Mythological animals and animals that did not fit conventional patterns in nature were given special symbolic significance, could traverse in more than one nonordinary realm, and were believed to own other animals or forms of nature, such as trees, plants, and springs.[1] A curanderx could connect with an animal associated with a specific nonordinary realm during a trance journey to deepen their connection with that animal or gain access to the realm. They journeyed into these realms via dreams, at natural and constructed sacred spaces—

where the veils of reality were thin—through ritual performances and costuming, and through the use of sacred tools, such as breathwork, entheogens, bloodletting, trance dancing, and playing and listening to repetitive drumbeats.[2] Wearing or including a sacred item of an animal—feathers, a piece of fur or skin, or their blood or teeth—or carrying an image of the animal strengthened the link and also provided a gateway into these realms.

The cardinal spaces were also sacred entities in their own right and had their own forms of divine wisdom, sacred gifts, patrons, deities, day signs, and year signs. Their symbols, meanings, and purposes, however, often varied among the ancient Mesoamericans.[3] The types of animals and animal deities that presided over and were associated with the cardinal spaces and their divinatory day signs were significantly more disparate throughout ancient Mesoamerica than the animals in the nonordinary realms. There were also myriad factors that could alter the meanings and understandings of their animal day signs, such as the numbered coefficient* related to that day sign, the year bearer sign that influenced the day sign, and, of course, the curanderx's own particular training in performing divination. The discussion of the animal day signs and their associated cardinal spaces will be fleshed out in the second part of the book dealing with the symbolic discourse and mythologies of the particular animal.

There were much more pervasive and resilient understandings throughout ancient Mesoamerica of the characteristics and attributes that connected an animal to a nonordinary realm and vice versa than to a cardinal space. Learning and connecting with animals in their symbolic habitat, the nonordinary spirit realms, is a very effective way of developing spiritual connections and symbolic communication systems with our animal spirit guides. Here, we can begin to transcend the

---

*A day sign could be tempered by the number it was assigned in the repeating cycles of one to thirteen, which also had specific assignments such as good, bad, neutral, and in between.

limitations of traditional, typically linear forms of communication and flow with and continue to develop our intuition. This is particularly true if we allow ourselves to open up and tune in to see and understand their various skills, talents, and medicine and how they like to communicate and interact with us. Accessing the nonordinary realms with an animal spirit guide or by shapeshifting into an animal can also provide a more graceful, safe, and exciting journey into these realms and allow us to go deeper into our journey to access the medicine there and bring it into our everyday lives.

ACCESSING THE NONORDINARY REALMS THROUGH TRANCE STATES

We can access the nonordinary realms by inducing a trance state, also known as a shamanic state or altered state. The following sections provide some of the ways to do this.

Auditory Stimulation

Rhythmic, repetitive, auditory stimulation using a drum, rattle, singing bowl, or even nature sounds can cause changes in the central nervous system and create visual stimulation of color, pattern, and movement, which are ideal for trance states. Tibetan and crystal bowls, particularly, affect the electrical activity in many sensory and motor areas of the brain.

In the classes I teach on working with and connecting with animals, my husband will usually play the gongs and Tibetan and crystal bowls and sometimes have animal nature sounds in the background. I tend to use the rattle and drum. Drumbeats are of low frequency and transmit impulses along a variety of neural pathways to induce trance states.[4] The drum also links the human heart with the heartbeat of the earth. The beats should be strong, monotonous, unvarying, and rapid. There should be no contrast in intensity or in the intervals between them.

At first, you may need to hear a recording or have someone playing the drum, rattle, or Tibetan bowl to induce a trance. But the more we practice and train our brains to go into trance states, the easier it becomes to induce them.

Shamanic Breathwork

Various types of shamanic breathwork exercises can induce particular trance states. Some can calm and quiet the monkey mind, while others can make us feel a restorative energy that enables us to journey into the nonordinary realms. The breathwork exercises I choose for particular journeys complement the intended journey.

Acupressure Points

Acupressure points are points in the body that are connected to its subtle energies. When pressed upon, they stimulate the body's natural self-curative abilities by releasing muscular tension and promoting the circulation of blood. Certain acupressure points stimulate particular areas and correlating energetic systems, enabling us to enter specific nonordinary realms.

Mudras

Mudras are hand, body, or facial postures that act as catalysts for speeding up electromagnetic currents and affect the subtle bodies. Like acupressure points, they stimulate particular areas and correlating energetic systems that enable us to go into specific nonordinary realms. We will be working with facial and hand mudras.

Toning

There are certain sounds that are experiences of energy in their own right. The sounds and *bijas* (seed mantras) I suggest using do not represent things or concepts; rather, they are energetic frequencies that stimulate particular areas and correlating energetic systems that enable us to go into specific nonordinary realms.

Shamanic Dancing and Movement

To facilitate trance journeying, it is also very helpful to have a combination of physical and mental meditative activities that help move any stuck or tense energy in the body that may impede the journey. Mental activities include prayer and visualization. Physical exercises include shamanic dancing, yoga, balanced movement, qigong, tai chi, contemplative walks, and the primal releasing breathwork.[5]

ANIMALS OF THE UPPERWORLD

For the ancient Mesoamerican peoples, the Upperworld was typically linked with the sky and cosmos. It was where animating energy was stored and emitted. It was a space that could be observed for divinatory purposes to better understand the activities of the deities, ancestors, and supernatural beings and to discern when to perform certain rituals. The Upperworld was also where the idealized processes of rebirth and resurrection took place and where supernatural beings, nobles, brave warriors, and the virtuous resided.[6]

The Upperworld of the Central Mexican peoples was divided into thirteen ascending levels, although a few sources indicate a division of nine or twelve.[7] Each level had and emitted different aspects of animating soul energies. Vatican Codex A provides a description of the various levels of the Upperworld. The lowest one was the one that was visible to all. It was the realm where the moon and clouds traveled. The second level was Citlalco, the place of the stars.[8] The third level was the one in which Tonatiuh, the sun deity, resided.[9] The fourth was Ihuicatl Hhuiztztlan, the place where Venus (Citlalpol) could be seen. The fifth was the level of the comets, the smoking stars or meteors (citlalin popoca), an immediate source of *tonalli*.* The sixth and seventh levels were the levels of night and day, where only the colors green and blue

---

*As I explain in the next chapter, unlike the two other soul animating energies, tonalli was transferrable in the sense that it could be lost or stolen without complete cessation of life.

could be seen, or alternatively black and blue. The eighth level was the place of storms. The ninth, tenth, and eleventh levels were the dwelling places of the gods. The twelfth and thirteenth comprised Omeyocan, the place of duality, the source of generation and life, the primordial dwelling place of their principal creator deity, Ometeotl.[10]

The Maya Upperworld was also divided into thirteen ascending levels that were associated with different planets, deities, comets, and the sun. Although the specific dynamics of these thirteen levels are not yet fully understood, the books of Chilam Balam* and their artwork provide insight on these thirteen levels. According to the Chilam Balam of Maní, the moon was in the first, the stars were in the second, Venus was in the third, the sun and Mercury were in the fourth, Mars was in the fifth, and Jupiter and Saturn were in the sixth. The Chilam Balam of Kaua placed Venus in the third and the sun in the fourth level.[11] In artwork, the sun and moon were often depicted along a double-headed serpent that represented the ecliptic and traced the annual motion of the sun across the sky. Interestingly, many of these same planets, deities, and natural phenomena had nocturnal as well as diurnal aspects, wherein they journeyed into or transformed and became lords and residents of the Underworld at night.

The most idealized level, a paradisal realm identified by many Mesoamerican scholars as the Flower World, was deeply associated with the Upperworld. For the Central Mexican peoples, brave warriors, nobles, and supernatural beings resided in this realm they called Xochitlan (the land of flowers) or Tonatiuhilhuicac. Four years after their death, brave warriors and nobles would be reborn as hummingbirds and butterflies, rise with the dawning sun in the east, and spend a joyful eternity drinking the nectar of flowers.[12] Hummingbirds were deeply linked with rebirth and the Flower World, likely due to their

---

*The books of Chilam Balam are the sacred books of the Maya of Yucatán; they are the most important source on the traditional knowledge of the Maya and early Spanish traditions. They were handwritten and are named after the small towns where they were originally kept.

torporific ability to protect themselves from the cold by lowering their body temperature and slowing down their heart rate to just a few beats per minute, which made them appear as though they had died and later come back to life.[13]

According to Diego de Landa, a sixteenth-century missionary and ethnographer, the Yucatec Maya also believed in a paradisal Flower World realm, where the deceased who had been virtuous would be in peace forever with an abundance of food, delicious drinks, and a refreshing and shady tree called the yaxche (ceiba) tree.[14] Mesoamerican scholar Karl Taube points out that this paradisal realm is likely the Flower World, which was ubiquitous in Maya art as both the dwelling place of ancestors and the mode in which ancestors and celestial gods ascended into the sky.[15] The Maya often portrayed the Flower World as a pyramid with stairways flanked with plumed serpents and flowers, which likely served as a symbolic passage into this paradisal Upperworld realm.[16]

The mythological feathered serpent and animals that were diurnal and could fly, jump great distances, and reside high in trees were identified with the Upperworld and its sacred gifts and medicine. The feathered serpent was accorded dominion over the Upperworld and Middleworld and had powers that were adopted and mimicked in many ways by the ancient ruling hierarchy. The feathered serpent was also a powerful symbol of transformation. Both birds and serpents share a common evolutionary origin as eggs and become divergent creatures.[17]

Perhaps because of birds' association with the Upperworld and the practice of observing phenomenon in the sky to divine into circumstances, curanderx often equated birds with being prophetic messengers.[18] Jacinto de la Serna, seventeenth-century ethnographer in Central Mexico, noted that the practice of watching the way birds fly, listening to them sing, and speaking to them continued to be a common practice throughout the seventeenth century for divining meaning or foretelling the future.[19] The Yucatec Mayan word *mut* means both "bird" and "augury," another indication that birds are seen as prophetic messengers.

High-flying birds with daytime hunting habits, such as the hawk, eagle, and falcon, were typically identified as manifestations of the sun and were linked with the Upperworld and brave warriors.[20] Birds with brightly colored feathers, such as hummingbirds, parrots, macaws, quetzal, lovely cotinga, and toucans were also often associated with the sun, the Upperworld, and precious elements, such as fire and water. Their bright feathers were believed to flash like fire in the bright sunlight and give off soul animating energy.[21] Nobles, rulers, and high-ranking curanderx wore brightly colored feathers to connect them with precious elements and to signify their high social status.[22]

There were also some terrestrial animals that were given cosmological Upperworld aspects because of mythological beliefs. The water turtle, for example, was associated with creation, the earth, and the constellation Orion. Orion was believed to be a place of cosmic creation, and the Maya paddler deities were thought to set their hearthstones in the starry turtle of Orion's belt.[23] Peccaries, often associated with fertility and renewal, were also associated with Gemini, which was immediately adjacent to that same three-hearthstone turtle constellation.[24]

The Sacred Gifts of the Upperworld and Its Animals

The following are some of the sacred gifts of the Upperworld and the ways that you can experience them. Please keep in heart and mind that these nonordinary realms may offer you different types of medicine, divinatory insight, or information about your soul's path. Listen to your intuition and use this list as a springboard to let you soar up into these realms and create your own path.

- ◄ Seek guidance from ancestors or other divine supernatural (earthly and cosmological) beings.
- ◄ Connect or retrieve soul pieces. Pieces of our soul that are in the Upperworld are residing there to obtain medicine for something that is too difficult to see the truth of, or someone or something we held on a pedestal and were let down by.

◀ Tap into the sacred energies of rebirth, resurrection, and creation.

◀ Connect with childlike innocence, bliss, joy, and happiness.

◀ Charge items and spaces with particular planetary or star energies.

◀ Access sacred essence energies from the sun and the cardinal spaces.

Here are some examples of Upperworld animals and a few of their gifts:

◀ **Hummingbird:** creation, death and rebirth, and love (refer to page 119 for more insight)

◀ **Feathered serpent:** metamorphosis, wisdom, and creation (refer to page 111 for more insight)

◀ **Eagle:** courage, strength, and discernment (refer to page 108 for more insight)

Accessing the Upperworld and an Upperworld Animal

The Upperworld can be entered through dreams, mountain caves, tree trunks, waterfalls, and visualizations of clouds, rainbows, one of the natural objects in our solar system (sun, moon, star, comet, or planet), and the paradisal Flower World. To access an Upperworld animal and Upperworld medicine, either you can choose an animal that is related to the Upperworld, which may be easier at first, or you can set the intention of journeying into the Upperworld and let yourself be open to whichever Upperworld animal is willing to work with you. If you decide to pick an Upperworld animal before you journey there, close your eyes and engage in slow breathing to see which animal calls to you.

You can also journey through the Upperworld as your I Am divine presence or shapeshift into an Upperworld animal. Our I Am is infinite and multidimensional, and it is also a shapeshifter and can be in many places and spaces at one time. (In the next section, I discuss how to merge and connect with our I Am presence.) In both scenarios, you can still have an Upperworld animal be your guide. If you go as an Upperworld animal and are new to shapeshifting practices, I recommend that you first start with developing your etheric shapeshifting skills (refer to page 52).

The areas of the body and energy centers, or chakras, that the Upperworld is typically associated with are the throat chakra (which can also be stimulated to access the Middleworld), third eye chakra (located at the center of the forehead), and crown chakra (located just above the top of the head). Stimulation of these chakras and areas of the body coupled with the element of intention can direct our consciousness into the Upperworld. You can use any of the methods listed above to enter a trance state or try the following breathwork sequence.

▣ Cobra Breathing

Start with Cobra Breathing to charge the body with life-force energy, as all trance journeying requires energy.

Position your hands according to the Cobra acupressure points: Cup your hands over your face. Place the index fingers on the temples and place pressure there. The middle and ring fingers should be slightly above the eyebrows. Place the pinky fingers at the bridge of the nose and put pressure there. These acupressure points also relieve most kinds of headaches and help us to become more focused, centered, and grounded.

Keep your hands in the Cobra position and take quick breaths in from the abdomen, while keeping the diaphragm contracted. Bring the breath to your chest each time. As you are breathing count to eleven, twenty-two, or thirty-three, and refrain from exhaling until you reach the end of your count. Counting to master numbers—eleven, twenty-two, or thirty-three, while engaging in this breathwork helps induce a trance meditative state. Which master number you choose to count to is irrelevant. After you count to eleven, twenty-two, or thirty-three, exhale through the mouth. Repeat this breathing exercise three times counting to eleven, twenty-two, or thirty-three each time.

▣ *Balancing into Higher Consciousness Breathing*

Inhale, hold your breath, and tighten all of the muscles in your buttocks and lower and upper abdomen, slightly curling in the spine. Hold your breath for about thirty seconds and envision a ruby ball of energy forming at your tailbone. Exhale slowly out of the mouth and allow the ruby ball to travel up the spine, slowly straightening the spine and bringing the ruby ball up to the top of the head. Repeat this at least three times.

▣ *Stimulating the Third Eye*

Position both of your hands in the *vayu* mudra: Press the tip of the index finger to the base of the thumb and wrap the thumb around the index finger. Let the other fingers stay straight. Now place your straight middle fingers directly between the eyebrows, in the indentation where the bridge of the nose meets the forehead, and place pressure on this point to stimulate the third eye. Inhale, then exhale with an "aye." Repeat three times.

▣ *Activating the Crown Chakra*

Position both of your hands in the active *guyan* mudra: Bend the first joint of the index finger under the first joint of the thumb, while keeping the rest of the fingers straight. Place your straight fingers underneath your earlobes at the indentation and put pressure on this point to stimulate the crown chakra. Inhale, then exhale with an "ee." Repeat three times.

Journeying into the Nonordinary Realms through Our Sacred Heart

Our sacred heart is the space where we can safely journey to the nonordinary realms, as well as to all dimensions, soul lineages, worlds, and realities—past, present, and future. Malina, one of my mentors, taught me to journey by going through *el sagrado corazon*, or the sacred heart. She explained to me that it was deep within the heart chakra. It is the space where we are the I Am presence, the divine presence within all of us, and we become and have access to infinite possibilities. Journeying within the sacred heart helps us release and transmute duality consciousness, fear, doubt, and other lower-vibration thoughts and emotions.

Before I guide you into this journey, I need to first state a paradox. Truly, there is no entering or journeying into the sacred heart. Rather, we are simply remembering that there is no separation between us and the divine and that we embody the divine. In this divine remembrance, "protection" from others is no longer needed on any level. As the divine, we choose what we allow into our space. We can simply set the intention of what we choose and know that this intention will hold.

Nonetheless, the ritual of journeying into the sacred heart always inspires deep humility, compassion, and love within me, so I always engage in this ceremony. I love it and hope you will too.

🔲 *Journeying into the Upperworld through the Sacred Heart*

Allow yourself to go into a gentle trance meditative state and slowly inhale through the nose and exhale through the mouth or nose, whichever feels more comfortable. Allow your heart to open up to you and thank yourself for gifting yourself with this space and time to become more self-aware and continuing your path of self-love and healing. Set the intention of journeying into the Upperworld and connecting with the divine presence within you, your I Am. If you are having trouble connecting with your I Am, a powerful and effective method for entering this space is both a command and a statement of truth: "Stand aside, ego, in the name of God.* I Am That I Am."

Allow your heart to continue to open up to you and love yourself even more. As you are opening your heart, imagine an emerald light streaming out from the center of your chest. At the other side of the emerald light is a mirror reflection of you (it could also be your I Am in an animal form or zoomorphic form), it is the you that is always encouraging you

---

*I use the term God to mean "divine love," free of any religious association. If you do not feel comfortable with the term God, use a word or concept that signifies pure divinity and consciousness to you.

to be patient, loving, compassionate, and tender with yourself first and foremost, so you can be more patient, loving, compassionate, and tender with others.

Now see your I Am become infinitely small, standing on a zero-point stream of light radiating from your sacred heart. Walk toward and into the sacred heart. The first gateway into the sacred heart is the violet fire of transfiguring divine love and infinite physical perfection. Allow the violet fire to completely encompass you, caress you, and love you. Place into it any lower emotions or beliefs that you are ready to let go of, especially fears and doubts. Allow yourself to remain in the violet fire throughout this journey, releasing stuff that you are ready to let go of, as well as things that may come up in the journey. The second gateway into the sacred heart is the white fire of purification and resurrection. Allow this white fire to also completely encompass you, caress you, love you, and inspire you to remember and become your infinite I Am nature.

As you walk within your sacred heart, visualize yourself in a beautiful floral paradise and call upon the Upperworld animal you have chosen to connect with or let yourself be open to an Upperworld animal. Imagine that this animal appears before you and telepathically let the animal know what medicine you are seeking from the Upperworld. Thereafter, journey with this animal and allow it to guide you or let yourself become this animal and explore the Upperworld in its form. If you are going to join and enter the body of the animal rather than shapeshift into its form, ask for permission first (refer to page 57 for more information on joining with animals). Let yourself also welcome in all the medicines that are ideal for you and are prevalent in the Upperworld.

After the journey, thank your animal guide for its help and see yourself being reborn first in the sacred white fire of purification and resurrection and then in the violet fire—seeing the violet-fire angels congratulating you for being vulnerable, brave, and bold and releasing that which no longer served you. Then take six deep breaths, inhaling through the nose and exhaling through the mouth. Gently rub your thighs with your hands, coming back fully present and grounded.

ANIMALS OF THE MIDDLEWORLD

The Middleworld was composed of the four cardinal spaces and a center as well as natural and constructed spaces that acted as portals to access the sacred energies of the cardinal spaces and the nonordinary realms and also provided doorways and homes for supernatural beings to enter or reside. People, curanderx and rulers in particular, could also act as metaphorical portals to the nonordinary realms, retrieving insight medicine and guidance from these sacred realms.[25]

Sacred natural spaces—including mountains, caves, forests, particular trees, ravines, anthills, edges of volcanoes, certain bodies of water, and generally intersections between two natural elements—could act as portals as well. For the Mexica, mountains were places where the paradisal Flower World could be found, as well as the dwelling place of the solar deity, Tonatiuh.[26]

The Mexica's capital of Tenochtitlan mirrored the spatial configuration of the Middleworld, with its four large quadrants symbolizing the four corner cardinal spaces and a ceremonial center.[27] The Great Temple, or Templo Mayor, consisted of four steplike platforms, one on top of the other, relating to the cardinal quadrants. The three lower platforms consisted of twelve sections; the thirteenth section was the small top platform where the dual temples of Huitzilopochtli and Tlaloc were located. These thirteen sections mirrored and acted as gateways to the thirteen levels of the Upperworld. The courtyard of Templo Mayor had four doors or entrances, one each at the east, west, north, and south.[28]

The terrestrial aspects of the Middleworld were also associated with renewal, fertility, seasonal changes (and changes in general), agriculture, creation, resilience, and the ability to give life.

Animals that could conceive numerous eggs and babies, such as rabbits, coati, frogs, toads, opossums, and peccaries, were associated with fertility and the creation of the Middleworld. These animals often had links to the Upperworld or Underworld, as well as the

Middleworld, or were associated with all three nonordinary realms. Rabbits, for example, were also associated with the Underworld, as well as the night sky, the moon, and pulque (a beer-like beverage made from the maguey plant), perhaps in part because rabbits burrow around the roots of the maguey plant and forage principally at night.[29] The gopher and coati's underground burrowing tendencies also gave them Underworld associations.[30]

Because frogs and toads can lay thousands of eggs and shed their skin, they were associated with the Middleworld's fertility and renewal aspects, as well as with the watery entrance to the Underworld, as they give birth in a watery environment.[31] Animals that had seasonal survival and breeding qualities, such as deer, were associated with the Middleworld but also had Upperworld realm associations due to mythological beliefs. Animals that could float on water such as caiman, alligators, and crocodiles were also depicted as a metaphor of the earth's surface, with each leg being a corner of the earth.[32] Their nighttime hunting tendencies and mythological associations as world trees and zoomorphic creatures also gave them Underworld and Upperworld associations.[33]

Animals that could be domesticated, such as dogs, monkeys, and turkeys, were also associated with the Middleworld.[34] There was, however, a belief that because of dogs' loyalty to humans and good nighttime vision they guided the dead through the Underworld.[35] Iguanas' resilience and ability to go four to five days without eating gave them Middleworld associations, while their mythological connotations also gave them Upperworld connections.[36]

The Sacred Gifts of the Middleworld and Its Animals

The following are some of the sacred gifts of the Middleworld and the ways that you can experience them. Again, I encourage you to allow yourself to be divinely guided and listen to your intuition as to what other gifts the Middleworld has for you.

◄ Use the portals to the sacred essence energies of the cardinal spaces and the sacred gifts of the nonordinary realms.

◄ Connect with or retrieve soul pieces. Pieces of our soul that are in the Middleworld are usually residing there to obtain medicine for something that happened in another point in our life or a past life.

◄ Tap into sacred energies of fertility, renewal, and creation of life.

◄ Learn how to be resilient and change with greater ease and grace.

◄ Gain access to bounty and abundance.

◄ Heal, rescript, and shift a situation that happened in our current life or a past life.

◄ Ground and balance ourselves energetically, mentally, physically, and emotionally.

◄ Gain wisdom from the earth and its elements.

Here are some examples of Middleworld animals and a few of their gifts:

◄ **Rabbit:** prosperity, fertility, and abundance (refer to page 140 for more insight)

◄ **Monkey:** creativity/arts, playfulness, and wisdom (refer to page 126 for more insight)

◄ **Opossum:** understanding, creation, and divination (refer to page 131 for more insight)

Accessing the Middleworld and a Middleworld Animal

The Middleworld comprises parallel earth realms that tend to look like literal or metaphorical places on the earth. In the Middleworld all of the earth's times and histories can be accessed and are essentially holograms, so time can be stopped to inspect and examine something further to understand, honor, and integrate lessons. The Middleworld can be entered through natural spaces (water, forests, caves, ravines, anthills, trees, edges of volcanoes, natural elements, and intersections between two natural elements), constructed spaces (temples, crossroads, entrances of buildings, hallways, staircases, and cemeteries), dreams, and sacred items (maps, medicine bundles, staffs, mirrors, stones, braziers, and minerals) that act as portals.

To access both an animal in its Middleworld terrain and Middleworld medicine, you can again first choose an animal that is related to the Middleworld, or you can journey into the Middleworld and let yourself be open to whichever Middleworld animal is willing to work with you. If you decide to pick a Middleworld animal before you journey to the Middleworld, close your eyes and engage in slow breathing to see which Middleworld animal calls to you.

Remember, you can go to the Middleworld as your I Am presence (which may look like a mirror reflection of you) or shapeshift into a Middleworld animal. In both scenarios, you can still have a Middleworld animal be your guide. If you go as a Middleworld animal and are new to shapeshifting practices, start with developing your etheric shapeshifting skills (refer to page 52).

The areas of the body and chakras that are typically associated with the Middleworld are the throat chakra (which can also be stimulated to access the Upperworld), heart chakra (which is located behind the sternum), and solar plexus (which is located between the navel and sternum and can also be stimulated to access the Underworld). Stimulation of these chakras and areas of the body coupled with the element of intention can allow us to access the sacred gifts of the Middleworld. Again, you can use whatever method you prefer to enter a trance state, including one of or more of the exercises above, or use the following breathwork sequence.

▣ Centering

Sit with your back straight. Place your hands in a prayer position at the center of the chest. Close your eyes. Pull the navel toward the spine, and take four inhales, sniffing three times in equal parts and filling the lungs completely on the fourth breath. With the navel still pulled in, exhale through the mouth, releasing the breath equally in three parts and emptying the lungs on the fourth exhale. Repeat this cycle for two to three minutes.

▣ *Activating the Solar Plexus*

Position your hands in the Maya Coming to the Surface mudra (a.k.a. Maya Power mudra): Make a gentle fist with each hand, and place your thumbs over the first digits of the index fingers. Place both hands against and between the navel and sternum on the solar plexus. Inhale, then exhale with an "oh." Repeat three times.

▣ *Activating the Heart Chakra*

Position your hands in the raising Maya mudra: Curl in the index, middle, ring, and pinky fingers to the first digit, and place these curled-in fingers against the center of the chest, while your thumb is straight. Inhale, then exhale with an "ah." Repeat three times.

▣ *Journey into the Middleworld*

Enter the Middleworld using your intention or couple the intention with the sacred heart entrance (refer to page 24 to review how to enter the nonordinary realms through the sacred heart).

As you walk within your sacred heart, visualize yourself in your favorite place in nature, preferably a place you have visited, and call upon the Middleworld animal you have chosen to connect with or let yourself be open to a Middleworld animal. Imagine that this animal appears before you, and telepathically let the animal know what medicine you are seeking from the Middleworld and that you would appreciate its guidance and any other insight it has as to a time and space you should visit for healing, understanding, or rescripting.

When you feel your journey is complete, thank your animal guide and exit the Middleworld through your sacred heart, seeing yourself immersed once again in the sacred white fire of purification and resurrection and then in the violet fire. Take six deep breaths, inhaling through the nose and exhaling through the mouth. Gently rub your thighs with your hands, coming back fully present and grounded.

ANIMALS OF THE UNDERWORLD

The Underworld was typically understood as a dreaded place of tests and tribulations and was associated with darkness, the night, the night sun, and the moon. At the same time, it harbored regenerative powers and at night emitted transformative energies. It was believed that the sun deity journeyed into the Underworld at night, shapeshifted into a jaguar, and resurrected at dawn once again.[37]

The Central Mexican peoples believed that the Underworld comprised nine levels, eight of them below the earth. Most people who died of natural causes, diseases, accidents, or other circumstances not specified by the gods inhabited the Underworld.[38] In their human creation myth *Leyenda de los soles* (Legend of the Suns), Quetzalcoatl, a deity of creation and wind, was required to journey into the Underworld to retrieve the bones of humans from the previous world. The devious Mictlantecuhtli, the principal lord of the Underworld, agreed to give up the bones but required Quetzalcoatl to undergo tests, which included blowing music from a solid conch shell. With the help of some worms and bees, he successfully passed the tests, obtained the bones, and ran off with them. Eventually Quetzalcoatl returned the bones to Tamoanchan, the place of origin, where Cihuacoatl, a mother earth deity, ground them into a flour-like meal on which the gods then shed drops of their blood to create the present race of humans. Due to his success in passing the tests of the Underworld, new life and beginnings were forged.[39]

The Maya believed that the Underworld consisted of nine levels beneath the earth. The entrance to the Underworld was a watery place that could be entered at the crossing of two rivers, through caves, bodies of standing water, and dark wild places, such as forests.[40] In the Popol Vuh, a sixteenth-century K'iché' work comprised of creation myths, legends, history, and ethical teachings, the Underworld is depicted as a watery realm or an actual body of water and as a source of transformation and resurrection. The mythical Hero Twins go through a series of tests that appear to be metaphors for overcoming illness and death. As a ploy to trick the Underworld lords, the bones of the twins are ground up like cornmeal and then thrown into a river. The faith and heroic deeds of the Hero Twins are rewarded, and they are resurrected as handsome boys and eventually defeat the lords of the Underworld.[41]

Animals associated with the Underworld included animals that were aquatic, meaning they could reside in or dive into water. Many waterbirds, such as diving ducks, geese, and swans, were associated with all three nonordinary realms due to their ability to fly and journey into the Upperworld, their associations with rain and the fecundity of the Middleworld, and their ability to dive into the waters of the Underworld.[42] Fish and fish-related rituals often had to do with the resources and bounty of the earth, as well as the regenerative powers of the Underworld.[43]

Animals that were consistently in darkness or were nocturnal, such as foxes, coyotes, opossums, raccoons, tapirs, centipedes, bats, owls, rats, fireflies, spiders, ocelots, pumas, and jaguars, were also linked with the Underworld.[44] Many of these animals were admired and feared at the same time because of their keen hunting prowess, or they were poisonous and by extension were associated with death, transformation, and regeneration. They were often depicted on Classic Maya vases as zoomorphic beings that appeared to give access to more insidious types of magical practices, sending soul or fatal illnesses to others and likely garnering others' soul animating energies.

The physical attributes of the nine-banded armadillo, as well as their digging tendencies and inclination to eat insects that reside in in-between spaces—chiefly ants and termites—linked them to the Underworld and its nine levels.[45] Animals that resided in in-between spaces or underground, such as rats and gophers, were also associated with the Underworld.

In addition, there were mythologies that connected animals with the night sky and by association, the Underworld. In the Dresden Codex, the Starry Deer Caiman/Crocodile is deliberately sacrificed to destroy the world and revive it.[46] It is a nocturnal manifestation of a celestial monster that symbolizes the Milky Way and is a consistent actor in Maya creation myths and the formation of the cosmos.[47]

The Sacred Gifts of the Underworld and Its Animals

Much of the time, people tend to shy away from the Underworld and its sacred gifts. But it is in this space where we do most of our shadow work and release toxic energies weighing us down, including self-imposed limitations, insecurities, negative habits, attachments to victim stories or identities, and many other unhealthy tendencies or characteristics. While many of the Underworld animals are feared, they can in turn aid and connect us with medicine to shift these toxic energies, patterns, and habits out of our lives. The following are some of the sacred gifts of the Underworld and the ways that you can experience them:

◄ Absorb its regenerative powers, if we do indeed move forward with releasing toxic energies weighing us down.

◄ Take advantage of the transformative energies it emits at night.

◄ Allow it to inspire persistence, courageousness, and humility.

◄ Understand, work with, and heal our shadow aspects.

◄ Connect with or retrieve soul pieces. Understand what we need to release, so we can welcome back home our lost soul pieces.

◄ Work with the earthkeepers to determine in which realm a missing soul piece may be residing and be granted safe passage into another lifetime or another point in our current lives to work with a soul piece. Animals of the Underworld are very familiar with its terrain and can lead us to these earthkeepers.

Here are some examples of Underworld animals and a few of their gifts:

◄ **Bat:** adaptability, release, death, and revitalization (refer to page 85 for more insight)

◄ **Coyote:** cunning, resourcefulness, and creativity/the arts (refer to page 96 for more insight)

◄ **Jaguar:** transformation, courage, and strength (refer to page 122 for more insight)

Accessing the Underworld and an Underworld Animal

The Underworld is a space where we can learn about and work with our shadow aspects and realize the courage to release toxic energies. Similar to the Middleworld, the Underworld can be entered through natural spaces (water, forests, caves, ravines, anthills, trees, edges of volcanoes, natural elements, and intersections between two natural elements) or constructed spaces (temples with nine doors—especially if spaced on the opposite side of a ball court—tombs, underground chambers and passageways, crossroads, and cemeteries), dreams, and sacred items (maps, medicine bundles, staffs, mirrors, stones, braziers, and minerals) that act as portals.

You can begin by either first picking an Underworld animal you would like to work with or seeing which Underworld animal comes forth to work with you. Also remember that you can go to the Underworld as your I Am presence or shapeshift into an Underworld animal and in both scenarios still have an Underworld animal be your guide. If you go as an Underworld animal and are new to shapeshifting practices, start with developing your etheric shapeshifting skills first (refer to page 52 for more information).

The areas of the body and chakras that are typically associated with the Underworld are the solar plexus (which can also be stimulated to access the Middleworld), the sacral chakra (located just below the belly button), and the root chakra (located at the base of your spine). Use whatever method you prefer to enter a trance state, including any of the exercises given above, or use the following breathwork sequence. If you have your own set of shamanic breathwork exercises, try to use the ones that purify, raise energy, and ideally also release adrenaline. It is very helpful to have a little adrenaline coursing through us when we are facing aspects of ourselves that may not be pleasant.

▣ Purifying with Breath of Fire

Sit on the floor in Butterfly Pose, with the spine straight and the soles of the feet touching so the legs are in a diamond shape, or cross your legs in a comfortable position with the feet underneath the opposite knees. (If neither of these is an option for you, sit in a chair where your spine can be straight.) Quickly breathe in and out through the nose, pushing the abdomen out during the inhalation and pulling it in during the exhalation. (If you are unfamiliar with Breath of Fire, watch a YouTube video that demonstrates how to do it.) Continue Breath of Fire for thirty seconds to a minute, or longer, and interweave this breathwork exercise with the next facial mudra.

▣ Raising Adrenaline with a Facial Mudra

Take a deep inhale, and extend your tongue out toward your chin while engaging in a snorey exhale. Repeat sticking your tongue out with snorey exhales three times. Then, go back to Breath of Fire for thirty seconds and afterward repeat the deep inhales and snorey exhales with your tongue out. Repeat the cycle one last time, so you have done the Breath of Fire and tongue-out exhales for three complete cycles. This mudra—tongue down to the chin—is identified with various icons from different traditions that embody power and strength, including Huitzilopochtli and Tonatiuh, displayed at the center of the Sun Stone, and the Hindu goddess Kali, destroyer of illusions.

▣ Root Chakra

Position the hands in the Maya arrival mudra: Curl the middle, ring, and pinky fingers in toward the palm and leave the index finger and thumb straight. Press the index finger to the middle of the crease in the back of the knee. This acupressure point stimulates the root chakra. Inhale and exhale with a guttural "uh." Repeat three times.

▣ *Sacral Chakra*

Position the hands in the om mudra: Join the tip of the thumb and index fingers, while the other fingers are straight. Use the straight fingers to place pressure on the spot two fingers below the belly button. This acupressure point stimulates the sacral chakra. Inhale and exhale with an "oo." Repeat three times.

▣ *Journey into the Underworld*

Enter the Underworld through your intention or couple the intention with the sacred heart entrance (refer to page 24 to review how to enter the nonordinary realms through the sacred heart).

As you walk within your sacred heart, imagine yourself before a natural or constructed space associated with the Underworld, and walk into the Underworld. Now call upon the Underworld animal you have chosen to connect with or let yourself be open to one. Imagine that this animal appears before you and telepathically let the animal know what medicine you are seeking from the Underworld and that you would also appreciate its guidance on how to move through the Underworld and approach any obstacles with fearlessness and persistence and on anything else you feel would aid you.

Journey with this animal as your I Am presence or let yourself become an Underworld animal. Remember, if you are going to join and enter the body of an animal, please ask for permission first. Explore the Underworld and let yourself be open to whatever medicines or sacred gifts come forward for you. When you feel your journey is complete, thank your Underworld animal guide, exit the Underworld through your sacred heart, seeing yourself immersed once again in the sacred white fire of purification and resurrection and then in the violet fire. Take six deep breaths, inhaling through the nose and exhaling through the mouth. Gently rub your thighs with your hands, coming back fully present and grounded.

ANIMAL MEDICINE FROM
THE UPPERWORLD: MY JOURNEY

Our work with animals in their nonordinary realms can sometimes bleed into our "mundane" realities and provide us with medicine, guidance, and strength when it is needed. On one particular occasion I had hummingbirds provide me with the Upperworld medicine of lightness and strength and the message that I needed to be a peaceful warrior of light in a less than pleasant profane situation.

When we moved to our new home in Tujunga, it took about twelve different types of contractors to turn our half-acre landfill of rocks into a beautiful garden oasis that also housed an acoustically sound temple for our sound baths. The contractors I hired ranged from outstanding to incredibly problematic. Despite not having too many flowers at the beginning, the backyard was swarming with hummingbirds. In my trance journeys, I constantly found myself being nurtured by the Upperworld and always surrounded by a clan of majestic brilliantly colored hummingbirds, who were armed in warrior regalia. In my journeys, they were very playful, yet also very persistent and would zip right in front of me to ensure that I saw their warrior regalia and then do backflips. This would always inspire my heart with strength and lightness.

Toward the end of the landscaping and construction, my husband and I found that we were having problems with the temple doors. They kept getting stuck, and the contractors who installed the temple kept coming out to adjust them but did not replace the frames. This happened three times within a couple of months.

The fourth time the doors got stuck, I called the contractors for help again. I immediately got transferred to the owner of the company. Before the owner got on the phone, a clan of four hummingbirds appeared outside our large living room window and performed the same routine I saw in my journeys. Each hummingbird flew right up to me and then performed a backflip (without, of course, the warrior regalia).

When the owner got on the phone, I asked him to come and adjust our doors because we could no longer close or open them. The owner told me that he was getting tired of coming out and asked if my husband was handy. He told me that the door misalignment was not their fault, as it was "clear" that the contactors who placed the gravel for the temple did not properly compact the gravel. I reminded him of an email I had from one of his associates, wherein the only specification I was given as to the type of ground terrain that was needed for the temple was gravel. He then said he would call me back.

At this time, the hummingbirds' performance accelerated. Each hummingbird darted back and forth, came right up to me in the window, and engaged in backflips. Although I really did not want to, I knew I had to step up as a warrior of light and remind the owner of the company why they had a legal duty to properly address this issue. Through my phone I quickly reread my contract, then went to their website and read their express warranty. I also spent a few minutes looking up the legal elements of an implied warranty and related uniform commercial codes. Less than ten minutes later, I called the owner back and reminded him how patient my husband and I had been with them and why, under the express and implied warranties and commercial codes, the company had a legal duty to finally fix this problem once and for all. We were still giving them the opportunity to fix this issue rather than hiring another company and then sending them the bill. He agreed, and this time when they came out, they properly fixed the issue and replaced the doorframes.

I knew that my journeys into the Upperworld and my work with the hummingbirds there were inspirational for me and enabled me to stay focused and centered as a fair, yet persistent warrior of light. This was true hummingbird medicine.

2
Diverse Shapeshifting Practices and Their Many Benefits

There are many ways to shapeshift into an animal and numerous benefits that can be gained from doing so, including tapping into the animal's strength, speed, and stamina, as well as whatever types of medicine it has to offer; gaining insight from a pure primal space; and healing wounds in our etheric bodies.

The ethnohistorical records, mythologies, and artwork of ancient Mesoamerica indicate that curanderx engaged in divergent shapeshifting practices. I approach the analysis of these shapeshifting practices by examining their three most common animating soul energies and how they likely enabled different shapeshifting practices. It is important to keep in mind that some of the more prolific and skilled ancient Mesoamerica curanderx may possibly have practiced other types of shapeshifting methods and rituals, beyond the ones identified in this chapter. This analysis nonetheless intends to continue a critical trend in assessing these ancient shamanic practices from a standpoint that allows and makes room for fluidity and dynamism and is open to the likelihood that these ancient curanderx used their animating soul energies to engage in diverse types of shapeshifting practices beyond just physical shapeshifting.

ANIMATING SOUL ENERGIES AND ANCIENT MESOAMERICAN SHAPESHIFTERS

Ancient Mesoamerican peoples generally believed that the body was a reflection of the earth, the cosmos, and the divine, as well as a receptacle for animating energy that originated outside the body and circulated throughout the cosmos.[1] These animating energies comprised the soul and its diverse manifestations and associations.[2] It was the means by which innate life force increased and had the power to make organisms come into being, live, grow, and reproduce. It also enabled different types of shapeshifting practices.[3]

The three animating energies were believed to be concentrated in the heart, head, and liver or stomach.[4] Although the ethnohistorical records on the Maya do not provide as much detail with regard to their bathing rite ceremony, we know that during the baby bathing rite ceremony of the Mexica, when a child's name and fate were divined by the *temixiuitiani, tietl,* or *tlamatqui* (midwife), these were the particular areas of the body that the midwife requested deities to cleanse, purify, increase, and infuse with their animating soul energy.[5]

These energies could be externalized in the following ways:

◄ Emitting divine energy through different types of shapeshifting performances

◄ Imposing one's will as animating soul energy on an element or different being*

◄ Invoking the aid of an element or other divine force via animating soul energy

◄ Physically shapeshifting into an element or different being

---

*In the categories of beings and divine forces, I include animals in general, animal coessences, and animal spirit guides.

◄ Taking possession of an element or different being

◄ Physically bilocating (being in two places at one time) as an element or different being.

The Central Mexican peoples called those who could will shapeshifting *nahualli*.[6] Bernardino de Sahagún, a sixteenth-century ethnographer, notes that there were *nahualtin* (plural of nahualli) that had the ability to shapeshift into animals, people, and natural forces such as fire, mist, vapor, water, rainbows, comets, lightning, and air, and some that could take possession of living people and animals. A nahualli could also shapeshift, see through, work in alliance with, and take possession of an animal they shared a tonalli with.[7] If something detrimental happened to the animal that the nahualli had shapeshifted into, regardless of whether it was their animal coessence or some other animal, the nahualli could be hurt or die in the same way.[8] A nahualli was typically born under the sign of One Rain (Ce Quiahuitl) or the sign of One Wind (Ce Ehecatl).[9]

The Maya had numerous names for their curanderx shapeshifters. The colonial Yucatec Maya, for example, had the following identifications for curanderx that could shapeshift at will: *ah uay balam*, a curanderx who could take the form of a jaguar; *ch'a-uay-tah*, a curanderx that could take the form of another *dzutan*, a curanderx that could take the form of a wolf; and *ah uay miztun*, a curanderx that could take the form of a cat. Curanderx that could charm or attract animals were called *ah cunal can* and *ah paycun*.[10]

The ethnohistorical records indicate that there were some adept rulers that also engaged in physical shapeshifting practices. The sixteenth-century ethnographer and missionary Juan de Torquemada indicates that rulers of the Aztec empire Tzutzumatzin and Motecuhzoma Xocoyotzin were nahualtin and could shift into many forms.[11] Tecun Uman, one of the last rulers of the K'iché' Maya in Guatemala, was also reported to have shapeshifted into a macaw and then an eagle when he fought against the Spaniards in 1524.[12]

The hieroglyph that has been associated with shapeshifting practices for the Classic Maya in particular is the T539 logogram: *way*, *wahy*, or *wahyis*. Marc Zender, a Mesoamerican scholar, determined that the use of *is* at the end of *wahy* is likely dealing with an absolutive suffix suggesting that the Maya saw animating soul energies, including spirit companions and animal coessences, as a subcategory of a body part.[13] The way glyph consists of a stylized human face, or possibly an *ajaw* face (the ajaw face was often depicted as two dots for eyes and a third dot at the bottom for the mouth), partially covered by jaguar skin. The root of *way* is the word for "sleep" in many Maya languages and has various semantic extensions, including dream, witchcraft, nagual, animal transformation, and other spirit or animal coessence.[14]

When first analyzed by Mesoamerican scholar Nikolai Grube and also independently by Stephen Houston and David Stuart, the way hieroglyph was identified with an animal coessence of a supernatural being or human.[15] The associations of the way glyph have been expanded to include natural sites having their own animal coessence; a person shapeshifting into other forms, including an animal coessence, other noncoessence animals, people, and natural forces; sending soul illnesses or diseases to another as a way; or acquiring another's animating soul energies.[16] Skilled warriors were also thought to channel and engage in some form of shapeshifting to gain a greater advantage over their opponents in battle.[17]

Heart-Centered Animating Energy

The heart was one of the areas of the body where a particular type of animating soul energy was concentrated. The Central Mexican peoples identified this energy as *teyolia*, *toyolia*, or *yolia* and associated it with sustaining life and making one live.[18] It vitalized and shaped thought processes and emotions; was responsible for affective states, abilities, and identity; and provided individual characteristics, such as personality, aptitudes, vocational abilities, and desires. This animating energy was a constant in one's life and could not be taken without complete cessation of life or breath.[19]

According to the Popol Vuh, it is in the heart that the mother and father of creation place their animating soul energy and give life. It states that the mother and father were the "giver of life" and the "giver of heart." The "creation [wa]s to be under the direction of its heart sky." In regard to "giver of heart," translator Allen J. Christenson explains in a footnote that the heart is understood as the central defining essence of a person, or what might be referred to as the soul. Thus, the creators are those who ensoul living things; it is the heart into which they place their animating soul energy.[20]

The Central Mexican peoples thought of this energy as a divine fire within the heart that could be increased by performing extraordinary acts in war, art, government, or other valued social expressions.[21] People who had achieved exceptional distinction in divination work, the arts, poetry, or intellectual pursuits were called *yolteotl* (deified heart) because it was believed that their hearts had received a divine force.[22]

According to the Central Mexican peoples, the following could cause damage to this animating energy: immoral conduct, heart conditions that were accompanied by phlegm in the lungs, and curanderx known as *teyollocuanime* and *teyollopachoanime*, who could magically devour or cause damage to this animating energy. The most common way to heal this animating energy was to have a *platica* (heart straightening talk) ceremony. The injured person would go to a *cihuatlamacazqui* (female curandera) or *tlamacazqui* (male *curandero*) and relay their wrongdoings to them to eject this energy from their hearts and bodies. Through her curanderx, Tlazolteotl, the deity of both restoration and filth, was believed to remove people's impurities during the platica, returning the heart to its proper place from which it had been dislocated.[23]

Just as this divine fire within the heart could be increased, it could also be emitted during sacred performance ceremonies. People who embodied divine forces during sacred performances could transmit this animating energy as a gift to their community.[24] Interestingly, Friar Bernardino de Sahagún alludes to some kind of shapeshifting in his descriptions of the sacred performances of the Ochpaniztli and

Tititl festivals. Sahagún indicates that after a *teccizquacuilli* (male curanderx), whom he describes as very strong, powerful, and tall, donned the garb and ritual accoutrements of the grandmother deity Toci, he embodied the third-gender aspect of Toci and thereafter was identified as a female.[25] In the Tititl festival, after a ritual dance called the *ilamatecuhololoya* (Ilamatechtli's leap), they adorned a male curanderx with the mask of Cihuacoatl, and thereafter he was identified as a female and embodied the third-gender aspect of this mother earth warrior deity.[26]

During the Pachtontli rite, when the third-gender aspect of deity Xochiquetzal honored the Mexica with her appearance and began to stage a prophetic weaving performance, master craftsmen disguised as monkeys, ocelots, dogs, coyotes, mountain lions, and jaguars reveled in a jubilant dance.[27] Whether or not these performers physically shapeshifted into any of these divine beings, the interviewees who relayed their performances to the ethnographers believed that some kind of energetic shapeshifting took place, wherein the performers shapeshifted into the embodiment of these divine beings. This was likely the very divine fire animating energy that the performer emitted and that contributed to their energetic shapeshifting.

Head-Centered Animating Energies

The second type of animating soul energy was concentrated in the crown of the head, hair, forehead, face, fingernails, blood, and joints and helped to synchronize the mind and body.[28] For the Maya, particularly the Classic Maya, *k'uhul* referred to sacred animating energy that emanated from deities and the cosmos and was depicted in glyphs of fragrant blossoms, breath volutes, jade beads, bones, shells, color signs, zero signs, maize kernels, and mirrors.[29] The souls of the dead were believed to depart from the head as a final flowery breath. Ears, along with mouths and noses, were often depicted as portals that emitted and received sacred life-force energy within the body.[30] Warriors and supernatural beings were often shown with flowers on their brows, suggesting the concentration of animating energy here. Through bloodletting, they used the blood's animating force to conjure their deities and ancestors, such as the vision serpents depicted in Lintel 24 of Yaxchilan.[31]

The Central Mexican peoples identified this animating soul energy as tonalli. As animating energy that permeated the earth, tonalli referred to many things, including solar heat, energy, or power. It also referred to a day sign of the 260-day *tonalpohualli* ritual calendar, which influenced a person's fate, destiny, or birth merit (*mahcehualli*).[32] The tonalli that was emitted varied qualitatively from day to day per the tonalpohualli cycle.[33] Along with the person's tonalpohualli day sign, various factors determined a person's type and degree of tonalli, including social class, age, and how well the individual preserved this animating energy.[34] People were careful to braid their hair to preserve their tonalli and ritually sunbathed to garner more of it. But they did so in moderation, as too much sun could have adverse effects. Remaining chaste until a person came of age was also believed to allow the tonalli to adequately develop.[35]

Unlike the other two soul animating energies, which were always a constant in the living body, tonalli could be lost or taken without complete cessation of life or breath and was likely the most transferrable energy among the living. Tonalli could be lost through sexual exploits, drunkenness, and interactions with people, particularly when they had an intimate connection with one another, such as family members. It could also be lost through fright and trauma, and it could be taken by people, typically sorcerers.[36]

Tonalli could leave the body during sleep and visit nonordinary realms, communicate with typically unseen forces, and acquire certain kinds of knowledge. It could also be lost due to a terrifying dream.[37] One of the many rites to restore tonalli involved startling the person by spraying blessed water on their face and then cleansing them with the smoke of the tobacco.[38]

Curanderx utilized their tonalli to shapeshift into animals. For the Central Mexican peoples and generally the Maya, social status, along with training, discipline, and skills, affected the types of animals they could shapeshift into.[39] Ancient shapeshifting practices that used the tonalli were often associated with shapeshifting into the species of one's animal coessence and were identified as *tonalismo*.[40] While shapeshifting into an animal coessence may be more intuitive, especially since both the curanderx and the animal share the same tonalli (as an energy signature), it is important to keep in mind that our other animating soul energies are also used to shapeshift into our animal coessence and that the tonalli can also be used for shapeshifting into animals that may not be our animal coessence.

Liver- or Stomach-Centered Animating Energies

The final animating soul energy was concentrated in the liver or stomach and was associated with the air in the body, as well as the release of it as breath, odor, and gas.[41] The Central Mexican peoples called this animating energy *ihiyotl*. In *Vocabulario*, Alonso de Molina, sixteenth-century missionary and ethnographer, lists many terms indicative of this animating energy and its force under the root of *ihi*. These include *ihiomotzaqua*, meaning to wrap up by my breath or to have the soul; *ihioana*, to attract something toward oneself through breath; *ihiocuitia*, to invigorate or feed another; *ihiocaua*, to weaken or to lack breath from much work or from illness; and *ihiomictia*, to stop the breath of another.[42]

As exhaled breath and speech, ihiyotl could serve as a forceful animating energy that could heal, work magic, manifest, persuade, or compel.[43] Control over this energy was tantamount to control over one's emotions, as ihiyotl was released during intense emotions. The origin of anger was attributed to the liver, which produced "thick, greenish-blue" bile during moments of intense anger.[44]

Ihiyotl was also believed to be released during the ritual speeches of rulers. Newly installed rulers would plead with deity Tezcatlipoca to strengthen their enchanting ihiyotl energy and to ensure that heat, warmth, freshness, tenderness, sweetness, and fragrance be exuded from their words.[45] Ihiyotl as breath was often depicted as sweet-smelling flowers. But it was also related to the foul odorous gases and vapors that were emitted by bodies and other objects, such as rotting foods and swamp gases.[46] The ihiyotl was also one of the principal animating soul energies used by nahualtin for shapeshifting practices.[47]

The Maya also identified the breath as an animating energy and closely associated it with substances that had ethereal qualities carried by wind or air, including the sweet aroma of flowers and copal, and sound, especially music.[48] Breath, or wind, was the food of the gods and ancestors, as well as what constituted their spiritual nature. The breath as animating energy could be pleasant and invigorating or toxic and possibly deadly, depending on whom or what it was coming from. The breath of royalty was depicted as fragrant and pleasing and likely intoxicating and influential. Rulers were often depicted with jade beads or flowers emanating from the nose.[49] The breath of the Maya lords of the Underworld in turn could induce illness.[50]

Based on the Maya's polychrome vases, lintels, and comparative ethnographic research it is believed that this animating energy was one of the principal energies used by Maya curanderx for shapeshifting practices as well.[51] This energy could also be used to send bad dreams and personified diseases and invoke demonic entities of the forest and underworld.[52] This energy as designated entities or animals could also be transmitted from one ruler to another within the same dynastic line.[53]

ANCIENT MESOAMERICAN PHYSICAL AND BILOCATION SHAPESHIFTERS

When Sahagún describes the diverse shapeshifting practices of the Central Mexican peoples involving animals, elements, people—alive and dead—and possibly even deities, it is not clear whether he is describing etheric, astral, physical, or bilocation shapeshifting practices or some other kinds of shapeshifting practices. There are, however, other sixteenth- and seventeenth-century ethnographers that appear to iden-tify instances of what is known as physical and bilocation shapeshifting practices. Greater details involving these shapeshifting practices were typically only provided when harm had come to the curanderx in their animal form. When both a curanderx and an animal were harmed or died at the same time and in the same way, it demonstrated the likeli-hood that these practices were real and therefore probably encouraged the ethnographers to document and relay them.

In the cases involving bilocation, the curanderx was conscious in their physical body as the animal merged with their primal animal instincts. In cases involving physical shapeshifting, the curanderx was involved in disparate activities, including healing a man, going into a covenant, and going to war with the Spaniards. In both cases, when something happened to the animal, the curanderx experienced whatever the animal form experienced. It was also often reported that in cases of physical shapeshifting, the animal looked slightly abnormal, was gener-ally larger in size, or simply had larger than normal features. Whether these practices of physical shapeshifting involved shifting into an ani-mal coessence is not clear, with the possible exception of Tecun Uman.

In the battle against the Spaniards, K'iché' ruler Tecun Uman was reported to have flown up into the sky as a quetzal before the Spaniards arrived. When they arrived, he became a larger bird, possibly an eagle. Conquistador Pedro de Alvarado, who was leading the Spanish army, threw a lance at Tecun, hit him, and killed him. It was said that Alvarado had cast a spell on his weapons.[54] Some stories report that Tecun shifted into his animal coessences, while others report that he was simply a shapeshifter.

Jacinto de la Serna reports of a curandero who healed people and could apparently do so as a dog. The curandero shapeshifted into a white dog and came into the house of an indigenous man who was sick, to help him. The wife of the sick man saw the white dog in their bed-room, did not recognize him, and went after him. She chased him and hit him with a stick. The white dog ran out of the bedroom. When the wife came out of the bedroom, she found the curandero who asked her why she had hit him and thrown him out of the bedroom and then told her that he was there to heal her husband, which he apparently later did.[55]

Ruiz de Alarcón reported another instance of a curandera, who could physically shapeshift into a bat, and who had been accosted by two missionaries in the convent of Santo Domingo. A bat came into the convent through a window that had been left open. When they saw the bat, the missionaries indicated that this bat looked abnormal and substantially older than most bats. They panicked and began throwing things at it, swinging at it, and trying to kill it. The bat escaped out the window. The next day an elderly lady came to the porter's lodge of the convent and asked to see one of missionaries. When he appeared, she told him that she was the bat that had been in the convent the day before and asked him why he had mistreated her and tried to kill her.[56]

Here are three instances of bilocation. One involves a fox and the other two, caimans. In the first, an indigenous man who was with a group of people began yelling, "Ay, they are killing me, they are chasing me, they are killing me!" The people he was with began asking him questions as to who was chasing and killing him. The man told them the name of the ranch where the cowhands were killing him. They went to the ranch and found that the cowhands had run down and killed a fox. When they returned to the man, they found him dead with the same blows and wounds that the fox had.[57]

In the second occurrence, an old woman who was sowing with another old woman said, "Simon Gomez has killed me," and suddenly fell dead. Simon Gomez was fishing in the Cachutepech River, near Acapulco. One of his two sons climbed onto a gravel bar that was in the river. A caiman came out and began to circle the gravel bar. Simon Gomez shot at the caiman and killed it, which is when the old woman fell dead. The woman's relatives filed a complaint against Simon Gomez, but Simon only admitted to killing the caiman, not the old woman.[58]

In the third incident, the priest Andres Giron was traveling with others to hear Mass in a settlement near Guatemala City. While they were crossing a river near the settlement they saw a caiman in it, and one of Father Giron's companions shot at it twice. One bullet entered the caiman's eye and the other its jaw. They hauled it out and scorched it with cattails and resumed their journey to Mass. When they arrived there was an uproar in the settlement's church. An indigenous woman had fallen dead at the time the caiman had been shot. This woman had one ruptured eye and a torn mouth. When they removed her dress, they found that her whole back had been scorched, as the caiman's had been.[59]

DEVELOPING SHAPESHIFTING PRACTICES

As the ancient Mesoamerican curanderx were aware, shapeshifting practices require the development, use, and mastery of soul animating energies. While shapeshifting practices can be learned and developed through these energies, there are some people that are more prone to be shapeshifters. Nonetheless, the more advanced instances of shapeshifting—astral, joining, physical, and bilocation—typically require practice and training. Although they are much rarer, there are still a fairly decent number of contemporary ethnographies that document these more advanced practices in indigenous towns throughout Mexico and Guatemala.

When I brought up the topic of shapeshifters, most of my mentors—with the exception of Don Fernando, who opened up to me quite readily—would initially look at me with a cautious eye and change the subject. When they got to know me, though, they too shared their shapeshifting encounters and experiences with me. I did not, however, take everything I was told at face value. After all, one of my mentors advised me to get rid of my beloved cat. According to him, all cats were evil. It turned out that one of the town brujas (witches) entered his house as a cat and tried to strangle his wife. I looked over at his wife while he was sharing this story. Her demeanor became very nervous and agitated, and she forced us off the subject. There was absolutely no way I was going to get rid of my furry daughter, but at the same time, I was definitely not going to challenge his strong feelings about cats. While this information comes from my mentors, it is also blended with my critical and intuitive nature, along with my tendency to do my own research.

In all of these shapeshifting practices, it is essential to have a high level of animating soul energy to sustain the shift and get the most benefits from it. It is also important to keep in mind that with all of these practices, especially when starting out, we tend to have an easier time shapeshifting into an animal that we feel a strong connection to. This is largely because when we feel particularly drawn to and can tune in to a particular animal, we can begin to take an etheric imprint of their body onto ours. The etheric body as we shall see is generally the first to shapeshift. As we become more familiar with and aware of our own energies and learn their degree of malleability, we feel more comfortable taking different forms and experiencing life through diverse kinds of animals, including mythological ones or even extinct ones.

I should also mention that because the full moon and the night sun* tend to emit transformative energies, engaging in shapeshifting practices on a full moon night is definitely helpful and conducive to these practices.

Etheric Shapeshifting

Etheric shapeshifting is the most common type of shapeshifting practice, as the etheric field around the physical body is typically the first subtle body in our aura to shapeshift. The aura is comprised of subtle biomagnetic energy bands (subtle bodies) around the physical body that

---

*Although there are variations, it was believed the sun entered the Underworld at sunset and became the night sun and was then reborn every morning at dawn. The night sun was believed to shapeshift into a jaguar and became a lord of the Underworld, while another aspect of the sun endured the tests of the levels of the Underworld. The night sun emitted transformative animating energy, as he journeyed through the Underworld at night.

are hierarchical in organization and vibration and graduate in frequency and color as they move outward from the body. These subtle bodies are connected to the physical body and its energy system (meridians, chakras, energetic core, and soul animating energies) and reflect and affect the things going on in both. The etheric, emotional, and mental subtle bodies are positioned closest to the physical body, respectively, and while what I identify as etheric shapeshifting may or may not involve all three of these bodies, it tends to always involve the etheric body.

The etheric body surrounds the surface of the body at a distance of one to two inches. It is an energetic mirror and blueprint of the physical body—giving it life and shape—and links it to the other subtle bodies. It also provides energy to revitalize the physical body and is involved in the process of physical healing.

The emotional body extends four to five inches from the body. It regulates our emotions and is often described as clouds that are typically in a state of constant flow, change, and movement, reflecting our emotional states. It carries the mind's translated information between spirit and body.

Finally, the mental body surrounds the surface of the body at a distance of eight to ten inches. Our mind interacts with etheric energy to create patterns in the physical dimension. It processes ideas, thoughts, and beliefs. It translates and directs information between the body and spirit, with the emotional body as an intermediary.

These bodies either collectively or in part can shapeshift into an animal. Etheric shapeshifting can happen spontaneously, especially while being in nature alone or with a person you feel absolutely comfortable with, in a deep meditation or trance journey, or in a dream. But at first, it typically takes practice for it to happen at all or to influence it when it does happen. If etheric shapeshifting does not come naturally, imagination is key in imprinting the animal onto our etheric body and shifting into it. Thereafter, if we allow ourselves to feel and think like the animal we are intending to shift into, then our emotional and mental bodies will also likely shapeshift. Generally, being around other people tends to impede this shapeshifting, as we may not feel comfortable allowing our primal instincts to reign.

When we engage in etheric shapeshifting, we open up to our pure and primal animal instincts and respond to the world in a way an animal would. Human tendencies—self-judgment, reservations, and limiting thought patterns and beliefs—are pushed to the background. Depending on the animal we are shifting into, we may feel a wildness or want to run for the pure joy of it. We may also experience emotional and mental expressions of the animal, and our human abilities, such as walking upright, using our hand dexterity, and having analytical conversations, may feel awkward and clumsy. Because our etheric body has shapeshifted, we may feel as though we have animal "phantom limbs" such as a tail, beak, muzzle, wings, paws, or animal ears. This shapeshifting cannot be spotted by most human eyes, but some people who have developed intuition or psychic skills may in some way sense or see etheric traces or imprints of the animal and the shapeshifting.

Etheric shapeshifting also allows us to experience the earthly planes and nonordinary realms as the animal we shifted into would. The more we are able to relax and balance our subtle bodies, the clearer our perception becomes and the more easily we can journey as an animal. Some would analogize this to remote viewing. I would agree minus any beliefs that we leave our physical body. Our animating energies are much more expansive than we believe, so rather than separating from our physical bodies, we can consciously expand out from them and engage in etheric shapeshifting. This approach is much more conducive to mastering and working with the soul-animating energies of the heart, which I discuss in the next section.

We can benefit greatly from etheric shapeshifting, as it allows us to do the following:

◄ Draw on the animal for strength, speed, stamina, agility, and whatever other particular types of animal medicine, skills, talents, gifts, abilities, and wisdom the animal has.

◄ Experience instinctual openness that heightens our senses and makes us feel more alert.

◄ Unplug from the analytical monkey mind.

◄ Heal wounds, tears, and dark spots in our etheric bodies.

◄ Adopt the animal's stronger immune system and gain immunity to particular illnesses.

◄ Experience the earthly planes as an animal would.

◄ Trance journey into the nonordinary realms and experience them as the animal we shifted into.

Astral Shapeshifting

Astral shapeshifting is a little more advanced than etheric shapeshifting and requires a greater degree of animating soul energies to facilitate. This shifting includes the etheric, emotional, and mental subtle bodies, as well as the subtle astral body. The astral body is about one to one-and-a-half feet from the physical body, follows the subtle mental body, and coincides with the fourth dimension—where time and space are no longer strictly linear, and the past, present, and future are much more fluid. It is the body of the soul's animating soul energies, wherein all actions, growth, and health of the physical body are prompted. The astral body contains all of ancestral-lineage, karmic, and Akashic Records. Immense healing, awareness, and realization can take place when we shapeshift via our astral body, as we can access other realities and heal past-life trauma; we are no longer bound by time-space continuum constraints.

Shapeshifting into an animal from the astral body is felt much more deeply: the animal's phantom limbs feel much more pronounced, and its talents, gifts, and proclivities become easier to access. During the journey as an animal we are also able to interact with the nonordinary realms much more deeply, have greater access to medicinal recipes and insights into particular occurrences, and can actually obtain an item from these realms. (One of my mentors obtained his physical *sastun**

---

*A sastun is an item such as a crystal or marble that provides divinatory insight and is said to be gifted to the curanderx by divine beings.

during one of his astral shapeshifting experiences as a jaguar.) We also gain access to other times and more fantastic surreal planes as an animal. Like etheric shapeshifting, astral shapeshifting typically cannot be seen, but some people who have developed intuition or psychic skills may in some way sense or see energetic traces or imprints of the animal and the shapeshifting.

Astral shapeshifting typically takes place when our brain is in one of the following brain wave frequencies: alpha, mu, theta, delta, or gamma. Each brain wave frequency, measured in cycles per second, or hertz (Hz), has its own set of characteristics representing a specific level of brain activity and a unique state of consciousness. But the brain fluctuates between states, emitting different patterns simultaneously, and we are seldom in just one brain state. Although gamma is the fastest brain wave frequency, I place it last because it is achieved by more advanced meditators, who are more conscious when going into deep meditations and shifting experiences.

◀ **Alpha (8–12 Hz):** Alpha brain waves are typically experienced when daydreaming, in a relaxed state, or right before falling asleep. This state is a gateway to the subconscious mind.

◀ **Mu (8–13 Hz):** Mu waves are most prominent when the body is physically at rest. Although alpha waves occur at a similar frequency, mu waves are present when we are visualizing ourselves engaging in a motor action.

◀ **Theta (4–7 Hz):** Theta brain waves are usually present in deep meditation or in a light sleep, including the REM (rapid eye movement) dream state.

◀ **Delta (0.5–4 Hz):** Delta frequency is the slowest of the frequencies. It is typically experienced in deep dream states and deep altered states. This state is often linked with healing, regeneration, and profound intuitive insight.

◀ **Gamma (25–40 Hz):** Gamma waves are the fastest brain wave frequencies. Unlike beta waves, which typically involve analytical reasoning and predominantly come from the left side of the brain, gamma waves are found in all parts of the brain.[59]

Unlike etheric shapeshifting, astral shapeshifting is typically induced by more advanced meditators. Some say that astral shapeshifting is analogous to an out-of-body experience. I feel, nonetheless, that how we approach these practices—separately (out of body) versus connectedly (within our subtle bodies)—can help us to further understand and work deeper with all of our animating soul energies, especially the energies of the sacred heart that to a large degree presume wholeness and inner connectedness. So again, when we astral shapeshift, we do not necessarily leave our physical bodies, we simply and humbly accept and own our truly expansive nature.

Astral shapeshifting can be beneficial because it allows us to do the following:

◀ Draw on the animal for strength, speed, stamina, agility, and whatever other particular types of animal medicine, skills, talents, gifts, abilities, and wisdom the animal has.

◀ Experience instinctual openness that also allows us to feel more alert on many levels.

◀ Do deep introspective healing of past lives, realities, and dimensions.

◀ Gain deep wisdom and insight.

◀ Heal ourselves on a soul level and do deep soul retrieval work by gaining insight from a purer primal space.

Joining Shapeshifting

Joining shapeshifting, or joining, is when we use our soul animating energies to project our consciousness into a physical animal. It is important to do this type of shifting with an animal we have a deep connection with and feel we have permission from. An animal we are not particularly familiar with may not appreciate having its body occupied, and it may react adversely and try to push us out. If we are violently removed from it or something happens to it, we can experience a loss or serious depletion of our animating soul energies. Asking permission from an animal to join with it is also the ethical thing to do.

When we join with an animal we are able to travel with it and experience the earthly planes through it. Joining, viewing, and experiencing life through an animal we have a deep connection with can be very healing, exhilarating, and revitalizing. When we join with our animal coessence we also experience a merging and expansion of our soul energies. To engage in joining, along with going into deeper brain wave states outside of meditation or a journey, which can happen, we must work on raising our soul animating energies, especially the energies associated with the liver, stomach, and solar, sacral, and root chakras, or what many Central Mexican peoples identified as the ihiyotl. These energies are needed to will our consciousness into an animal.

Joining can be beneficial because it allows us to do the following:

◄ Draw on the animal for strength, speed, stamina, agility, and whatever other particular types of animal medicine, skills, talents, gifts, abilities and wisdom the animal has.

◄ Experience instinctual openness that allows us to feel more alert on many levels.

◄ Experience soul retrieval or revitalization of our soul animating energies, especially if the animal is our coessence.

◄ See and experience nature and life from perspectives not normally available to us.

Physical and Bilocation Shapeshifting

Physical and bilocation shapeshifting are very similar. Physical shifting is when the physical body actually shapeshifts into an animal. This practice is rarer and practiced by more experienced curanderx. These people are typically born with a strong potential to physically shapeshift into a particular animal that the family shares a hereditary connection with. More skilled curanderx, however, are not limited to a particular animal; they can shapeshift into any animal, element, or even person. None of my mentors told me that they were able to physically shapeshift personally, but they did share their encounters with curanderx that were able to do so and what they knew about these practices.

Physical shifting can happen instantaneously or can be induced at will, which is generally a slower process. It takes a substantial amount of animating soul energies and food protein to induce or experience physical shapeshifting. Instantaneous shifters use substantially more energy than those who can shift at will. When animating energies have been depleted the shifter returns to their human body.

Bilocation shifting happens when a person *splits* their animating energies to take the physical form of an animal, while they are also in their physical human body. Once the animal body has formed, it contains the shifter's consciousness and personality. Some accounts claim that the person becomes unconscious during the bilocation, but while this may be the case for some shifters, many ancient and a few contemporary Mesoamerican ethnographies indicate that the shifters are conscious when they are bilocating. This form of shapeshifting is also very rare.

In both physical and bilocation shapeshifting, the solid matter of the physical body becomes partially etheric in nature—less physical and more like ectoplasm. The change happens fastest in the extremities— hands, feet, ears, and nose. When shifters are in their physical animal body, their animal and human etheric bodies are still present: the animal etheric body is the template for their animal form, while their human etheric body has become diffuse and stretched roughly over the animal body. The animal tends to look a little larger than usual and have hints of human characteristics. If the shifter is injured in their animal form, the person will be injured in the same way and region of their human body. Once the animal and person join back together, the shifter tends to have a clear memory of their ability to shift, of their time in the animal body.

Physical and bilocation shapeshifting can be beneficial because they allow us to do the following:

◂ Draw on the animal for strength, speed, stamina, agility, and whatever other particular types of animal medicine, skills, talents, gifts, abilities, and wisdom the animal has.

◂ Experience instinctual openness that allows us to feel more alert on many levels.

◂ See and experience nature and life from perspectives not normally available to us.

◂ Become more in tune with our energies.

USING ANIMATING SOUL ENERGIES FOR SHAPESHIFTING

All shapeshifting practices use various degrees of animating energies. I will use the Nahuatl terms *teyolia, ihiyotl,* and *tonalli* when discussing how to increase the level of these animating energies for shapeshifting purposes but draw from both Maya and Central Mexican understandings. While it is conceivable that a shifter may simply draw from their ihiyotl animating energies to engage in joining or their teyolia and tonalli animating energies to experience etheric shapeshifting, using a balance of all the animating soul energies will prolong the experience, allow us to get the most benefit from it, and enable us to feel an expansion rather than a depletion of energy, even after the shapeshifting.

All three animating soul energies are manifested in the breath and can be garnered through breathwork and other feats or ceremonies. In the following discussion, I principally focus on raising the energies to engage in etheric and astral shapeshifting, but raising these energies is, of course, essential to joining, physical, and bilocation shapeshifting as well.

Teyolia: Heart-Centered Energy

In this context, the heart is a metaphorical and physical center that acts as an energetic portal to other realms and is also where animating soul energy, particularly teyolia, emerges. Along with breathwork and energy enhancing movement such as qigong, tai chi, and shamanic dancing, the following are some ways to increase this type of animating energy:

◄ Engage in and acknowledge acts and practices of self-love.
◄ Engage in activities that incite pure creativity, particularly art-related activities.
◄ Do things you love and make you feel fabulous.
◄ Practice meditation and trance journeying by entering into the sacred heart (going through the violet fire and resurrection fire) and work through/merge with your I Am divine presence.
◄ Practice doing healing work for yourself and others by journeying through the sacred heart and doing the work in this space.

At least initially, I recommend engaging in any shapeshifting practice from the space of the sacred heart (refer to page 24). While it is not necessary to journey through the sacred heart, the ritual of journeying into the sacred heart raises teyolia energy and allows us to continue to tap into an infinite source of sacred energy.

Tonalli: Head-Centered Energy

Tonalli energy can be used in shapeshifting to help us remain more conscious, aware, and balanced during the process. Tonalli, among other things, synchronizes the mind, physical body, and subtle bodies. Engaging in soul retrieval processes and practices, such as the ones I outline in *Curanderismo Soul Retrieval*, along with shamanic breathwork and exercises that induce trance states and balanced states of peace, power, and serenity, help to raise our tonalli.

To utilize tonalli energy during the shapeshifting process, begin your journey through your sacred heart and then tune in to the balanced animating soul energy that permeates your body. See this energy blending and merging with your subtle bodies to shapeshift into an animal. If you are a beginner, start with the etheric body and stay with it until you feel it is time to move on to the emotional, mental, and then the astral bodies. I provide an example of a journey below.

Ihiyotl: Liver- or Stomach-Centered Energy

For all types of shapeshifting, ihiyotl is the energy that must be garnered and tapped into the most to experience more integrated (successful and balanced) shapeshifting. This is largely because it is a strong source of primal power energy that mimics the animating soul energies of animals and can incite the more advanced types of shapeshifting (astral, joining, physical, and bilocation). As exhaled breath and speech, it serves as a forceful invisible energy source that works magic, manifests, persuades, and compels.

Once you have entered your sacred heart and set the intention to balance your tonalli throughout your subtle bodies, and you feel balanced, at peace, and serene, then will the shapeshifting of your subtle bodies with your ihiyotl energies. In this process, start with your etheric body, and stay with it until you feel it is time to move on to the emotional, mental, and astral bodies. If you want to join with an animal that you feel a close connection to and you feel you have permission to do so, use your ihiyotl to will your consciousness into it.

Along with breathwork and energy enhancing movement (qigong, tai chi, shamanic dancing), the following are some ways to increase ihiyotl:

◄ Practice mastering the balance of your emotional and mental states.

◄ Engage in tantric energy exercises.

◄ Become familiar with your animating soul energies as will power and move them throughout your physical and subtle bodies through breathwork or other meditative practices.

◀ Keep your liver, stomach, solar plexus, sacral chakra, and root chakra healthy, strong, and cleansed. Keep in mind, though, that periods of fasts or liver cleanses are not ideal times to engage in shapeshifting practices for less than advanced curanderx. Wait until these cleanses are done, and your will power energy feels balanced.

◀ Sleep with an energy-generating crystal, such as a lemurian, quartz, or calcite, on your solar plexus, sacral, or root chakras (charge the crystal in the sun and moon for twenty-four hours before doing so).

◀ Lie out in the sun for twenty minutes (after applying sunscreen as appropriate) with an energy generating crystal, such as a lemurian, quartz, or calcite, on your solar plexus, sacral, or root chakras (charge the crystal in the sun and moon for twenty-four hours before doing so).

◀ Engage in empowering practices of public spoken-word performances.

◀ Work ethical, magical, or *limpia* rites and ceremonies.

▣ Trance Journey to Use Animating Energies for Shapeshifting

You can use these shamanic breathwork exercises or any breathwork exercises that help you to feel cleansed, balanced, and more cognizant of your energies.

Charging: Cup the hands over the mouth, and take a prolonged inhale through the nose. Open the hands, and exhale quickly three times through the mouth. Repeat three times.

Root chakra: Perform the root chakra Maya arrival mudra exercise from chapter 1 (see page 36).

Sacral chakra: Perform the sacral chakra om mudra exercise from chapter 1 (see page 37).

Solar plexus: Perform the Maya power mudra exercise from chapter 1 (see page 31).

Centering: Touch the tip of your tongue to the roof of your mouth and inhale through the nose for a count of six. Hold your breath for a count of six. Move the tip of your tongue to the bottom of your front teeth—the tongue is slightly outside the mouth—and exhale out the mouth for a count of six. Do this for three to five minutes.

Start the journey by moving your consciousness into your sacred heart (refer to page 24). Let your conscious breaths make you aware of the balanced energies within your body. Visualize your blood coursing through your head, neck, shoulders, spine, back, arms, hands, chest, abdomen, hips, thighs, knees, calves, and feet. Feel the balance, calmness, and even flow of the tonalli within your blood. Let this energy blend with and expand the internal sun within your abdomen/solar plexus region. See all of your animating soul energies blend, merge, and strengthen the spin of your chakras.

Expand this energetic resonance out from your physical body to your etheric body. Allow an image of an animal to come into your mind's eye, preferably one that you are attracted to and would like to shapeshift into. Visualize a glow of light around your physical body and your etheric body and let this glow of light take the shape of this animal. You can begin by shifting the extremities (hands, feet, ears, and nose) or simply allow the shapeshifting to begin to happen on its own. What gifts, talents, skills, wisdom, or abilities attract you to this animal? Imprint what attracts you onto your etheric body by setting the intention and then imagine yourself as this animal out in nature using and exhibiting these characteristics.

If you feel ready, strengthen the imprint by shifting to your emotional body and focus on letting yourself feel how the animal feels. What impulses, movements, actions, or gestures does this animal act out based on these emotions. You can then take it a step further by shifting to your mental body and focusing on what the animal acts out based on its thoughts.

Once you feel complete, see your subtle bodies shapeshift back into your human form. Then see yourself immersed in the sacred white fire of purification and resurrection and then in the violet fire, with the sacred fire angels congratulating you for releasing limitations and expanding your potential.

MIGUEL RELEASES ATTACHMENT TO HIS IDENTITY THROUGH SHAPESHIFTING

At some point during the first year my husband, Miguel, and I dated, we engaged in a private psilocybin mushroom ceremony. At the peak of this ceremony, grandfather mushrooms began to show my husband, who was my boyfriend at the time, that he was more than the identities— IT professional, son, brother, sharp dresser—he was clinging to. But this gravely concerned him. He turned to me and admitted that he was scared because he was not sure who he truly was. He then continued to insist on my telling him who he was. I continued to reassure him that his essence was pure love, and everything else was something he created and could recreate; there was nothing to fear in the malleability of identities and roles. I guided him out of a potentially bad journey.

My husband and I continued to grow together spiritually and about a year and half later, we had substantially more tools and engaged in another private psilocybin mushroom ceremony. A gorgeous incredibly large full moon was shining that evening. We acknowledged it and opened up sacred space by calling on the spirits of the cardinal spaces. We engaged in deep shamanic breathwork practices and then gazed into the moon and went into a journey. A while later my husband turned to me and told me that he had shed an immense layer of his attachment to identities and roles. Unlike the first time grandfather mushrooms approached him with these questions concerning identity and roles, he was no longer afraid and was willing to let go of his attachment to them. He told me that he felt his oneness and connection to everything and was ready to fully embrace that.

He then turned to me and told me that I knew what to do.

Although I had never done this before, I got up and knew exactly what to do. He was sitting down facing the moon. I went behind him and guided him to gaze into the moon and allow his breath to take him into the moon. I whispered to him, "Let go." I poured some of my personally crafted meditation oil into my hands, rubbed them together, and began to gently press my palms along his midspine. I saw his etheric body shapeshift into what looked like a bird. I joined him, and we flew to the moon together. Later he became a cat, and then a much larger feline. We allowed ourselves to etherically and astrally shapeshift into different kinds of animals for the remainder of the evening and had an incredibly great time. We had laid out various blankets and pillows in the backyard, and we ended up falling comfortably asleep outside next to our furry kids, Isis and Bagheera.

We woke up to a beautiful sunny morning. We had agreed to meet his family for brunch later that morning. Interestingly, although we had been vegetarian for over a year, that morning both of us felt an insatiable urge to eat meat, the rarer the better; something I had never done or craved, even before I turned vegetarian. Nonetheless, we both ordered a medium-rare steak.

When we got home after having brunch, Miguel and I integrated our beautiful journey. My husband admitted to me that he did not believe he would have been able to go as far he did had he still been clinging to the identities he was choosing to play. He knew he was more than these identities and roles; he was a divine loving essence. He further admitted to me that he had known this on a mental level, but our shapeshifting journey enabled him to understand and know this on a deeper soul level. We thanked each other for holding a beautiful sacred space for one another and closed our integration.

3
Developing Symbolic Communication with Animals

Developing symbolic communication systems with animals can be exciting and informative and help us to advance our spiritual growth and awareness. It can take place in the physical third dimension or in the nonordinary realms and can be used for many diverse purposes, including obtaining and understanding animals' spiritual counseling and guidance; seeing and comprehending more layers of a past, present, or future circumstance; and understanding our subconscious and unconscious primal instincts, fears, and desires. The development of this communication system presumes that we are doing so with an animal we feel some kind of spiritual connection to or an animal we feel we cannot ignore for whatever reason.

WAYS TO DEVELOP ANIMAL SYMBOLIC COMMUNICATION

An integral aspect in developing a symbolic communication method with an animal guide is courting: either we are courting them or they are courting us. Animals, like humans, are susceptible to energy and will pick up on when we are trying to connect with them, especially if we are enjoying it.

When we choose a way to connect with them, such as inviting them to guide us during our meditations, we place attention and energy toward this method of communication. They may then appear to us in our mind's eye or in the physical world with a message, when we are in the following meditative states of consciousness—taking a meditative introspective walk, sitting down meditating, or doing house chores while in a relaxed mindset. Trust that whatever method of communication you choose to use, it will be picked up energetically by an animal guide you have allowed yourself to open up to.

The process for developing animal symbolic communication includes the following techniques:

◄ Familiarizing yourself with the animal
◄ Gaining insight into the symbolic meaning via intuitive energy surges
◄ Developing intuition to comprehend symbolic meanings
◄ Practicing shamanic dreamwork
◄ Practicing automatic writing
◄ Becoming familiar with the animal's mythological symbolic discourse
◄ Strengthening the energy lines of communication

Familiarizing Yourself with the Animal

One of the most practical and useful methods for developing a symbolic communication is to learn about the animal—its physical attributes, natural habits, and instincts—and focusing on anything in particular that catches your attention. Look at pictures of the animal as well, especially those that show them doing whatever stood out to you in your research. The internet is a great way to quickly research the habits, appearances, patterns, and traits of animals and to start to discern what stands out to you about them.

Knowing the natural traits of the animal can often help you interpret and make sense of what you saw the animal doing and what it looked like and where it was when it was doing it. If you saw, for example, a nocturnal animal engaging in one of its typically nocturnal activities during the day, whether you saw it in a dream or a waking state, it is more than likely that the animal has an urgent message for you. Another example is if you saw an animal that looked larger in her belly than most animals that you saw in your research, it would then prompt you to find images of what that animal looks like when it's pregnant. If you confirm that the animal you saw was pregnant, then you know that it has a message for you concerning the birth of something.

While I may provide insight as to the symbolic meanings of animals in this second part of the book, I encourage you to focus on the animal's natural characteristics and what it is doing when you see it (however you may see it). I highly recommend doing this before you research the spiritual symbolism of the animal. Learning about the animal first typically helps to strengthen our connection and bond with it, allows the message it has for us to unfold in multifaceted ways, helps us trust our intuition and the messages we receive, and encourages us to develop our own modes of communication with our animal guides.

Animals are generally very telepathic. If they believe that you understand the message they are trying to convey to you, they will communicate with you substantially more and be willing to engage in more forms of symbolic communication to convey different messages. For instance, pay particular attention to what an animal is doing or carrying when it approaches you. If it is carrying something in its mouth, you can thank it for delivering a message to you, verbally or internally. Unless you have a different symbolic communication developed with that animal, the delivered message will be related to the symbolic meanings of that animal, which typically have to do with the animal's natural instincts and habits.

If you feel connected with the animal, you can ask it to deliver a certain message to you by appearing and doing something related to its natural instincts and habits. For instance, when I see a large flock of crows or parrots, I know they bring messages of abundance and great fortune—crows bring divine guidance and parrots fiscal-related abundance.

Gaining Insight into the Symbolic Meaning via Intuitive Energy Surges

To determine the message or purpose of an animal visit, whether it came to you in the physical realm, in a dream, or during a trance journey, try to intuit its meaning and see if you get an energy surge that what you are intuiting is right. Tune in to what emotions are triggered within you based on what you saw, and what you sensed about it. You can start by asking yourself what kind of feeling(s) the image of the animal elicits and what it was doing to incite that feeling(s) within you.

In this stage, you are simply gathering information, so don't censor it; just take it as it comes. For example, if you have a dream about an animal burying something, and you feel a strong connection to it, ask yourself what words or ideas come to mind when you think about what you saw. Here are some possibilities:

◄ The need to store or hide something
◄ The need to preserve something
◄ The possibility that something is being hidden

After you have invested some time in brainstorming on the incited emotions and associations of what you saw, go through them in a relaxed state and see which emotion and association combination triggers a lot of intuitive energy in you and provides a "yes" as to the meaning(s) behind what you saw and felt.

Symbolic messages are created out of energy whether they come forward in dreams, trance journeys, or something that transpires in our waking third-dimensional state. Tuning in to the incited emotion and association helps to make a connection to the energy source of the message. A surefire way to determine the essence of a symbol is to go where the energy is—connect it to the emotion and association that brings up a surge of intuitive energy.

Developing Intuition to Comprehend Symbolic Meanings

Purchase a journal or create a note on your phone that is exclusively dedicated to recording your symbolic meaning of animals. Include the date and time, as meanings tend to change depending on what we are going through in our lives. At the end of the journal, create a list of animals and their related symbolic meanings. Creating our own symbolic meanings for animal spirit guides enhances and personalizes our connection to the animals and encourages them to work with us more frequently.

When you are journaling, write in the present tense. Writing in the present tense can put you back in the dream, trance journey, or space you were in when you saw an animal spirit guide and allow you to recall more aspects of what you saw. If something profound comes to you, but you are in a hurry, write down keywords and bullet points. You can expand on them later.

Pay attention also to how the messages and counseling come through for you. Be aware of which intuitive skill(s) they come in through and the circumstances involved. This allows you to develop your intuitive skills and the manner in which you communicate with your animal spirit guides. Here is a list of the most common intuitive skills:

◄ **Clairvoyance:** the art of clearly seeing something or someone that is not physically present. Gazing* and developing our imagination are excellent ways to further open this channel of communication.

◄ **Clairaudience:** the ability to hear energy information. Hearing energy information can be experienced internally or externally.

---

*Gazing involves having our eyes one-tenth open and using a soft meditative focus to observe something.

External hearing involves hearing information that seems to be coming from an external source, such as hearing your name and looking around to find that no one is physically present. Internal hearing is similar, but the source is clearly coming from within; it's an inner voice that is speaking to you and relaying energy information. You'll know it is intuitive information versus random inner dialog, when it comes forward in a calm, yet persistent and consistent manner.

◄ **Clairsentience:** the ability to intuit (without thinking) the present, past, or future physical, mental, or emotional states of other people and environments. We can intuit what someone else is feeling or intending or whether they are ill, and we can better relate to others in general and avoid dangerous or stressful circumstances or environments. In this context, we simply sense the presence of our animal spirit guides.

◄ **Claircognizance:** the ability to tune in to the energy of the mind, the unconscious, and the collective consciousness. This intuitive ability comes through our mind as insight or inspiration.

Practicing Shamanic Dreamwork

Mesoamerican peoples believe that in dreams we travel to nonordinary realms, often through our tonalli. Dreams are experiences created through the interactions of the unconscious and conscious mind. The unconscious mind is a marvelous universe of unseen energies and forces, forms of intelligence that live within us. It is the secret source of much of our thoughts, feelings, and behavior. The unconscious mind manifests through a language of symbols. As we learn to read those symbols we gain the ability to perceive the workings of our unconscious.

An animal spirit guide can come in via our dreams and communicate to us through these symbols. Again, to understand the message, reflect on what the animal was doing and research its natural instincts and habits. To determine the message or purpose of the visit, see if you get an energy surge that tells you what you are intuiting is right. If the message(s) or purpose(s) is still not completely clear, simply be with your question(s) and invite the universe to help you become more aware of the answers as time unfolds.

If you feel you understand the message, before going to sleep or in a meditative state connect with the animal and thank it for its guidance and let it know you understand it. You can also write a letter or leave something on your altar or somewhere special and let it know you want to communicate more with it.

Practicing Automatic Writing

Automatic writing is another way to discover the meaning(s) behind what you saw an animal doing. Close your eyes, and take some deep breaths, inhaling through the nose and exhaling through the mouth. Open your eyes, and write down some of the possible meanings behind what the animal did and how they relate to the sacred medicine you were seeking from the nonordinary realm and your life. After you are done with this subconscious automatic writing dump, slowly read the meanings while taking deep breaths to see which meaning feels right; ideally it will be the one that gives you some type of energy surge. Once you have decided on the meaning, proclaim and share it with the animal. Close your eyes, imagine the animal in your mind's eye, and thank it for the message and the medicine it provided. The animal will more than likely appreciate your efforts to develop symbolic communication with it and will continue to appear in trance states—or in the physical realm if it is a local nonmythological animal—to grant the same or similar messages and medicine.

Becoming Familiar with the Animal's Mythological Symbolic Discourse

Knowing the mythological discourse concerning an animal can provide greater spiritual insight as to the meanings surrounding its visit, whether it was in a dream, trance journey, or some other incident. Many different cultures and traditions that have not interacted

with one another on the physical third-dimensional plane nevertheless share certain symbolic discourses within mythologies that reflect
similar understandings. These common understandings likely stem
from observing an animal's natural habits, attributes, and tendencies.
In some cases, the authors of mythologies also go beyond mundane
third-dimensional perception and tap into universal streams of energy
to translate and understand the multidimensional language of symbolism. The Mesoamerican animal mythologies I relay in an upcoming
section can help us do just that.

Strengthening the Energy Lines of Communication

When we begin to make an effort to learn more about our animal
spirit guides, they typically respond by making more appearances
in dreams, trance journeys, or the physical realm. To strengthen the
energy lines of communication with your animal guides, do any of the
following:

- Continue to meditate on or take a trance journey focusing and
  inviting them into your life.
- Place an image of them on your altar or in your office or home.
- If they leave a gift for you, such as a skin or feather, place this item
  on your altar or in a place you feel is sacred.
- If you see the animal in the physical, greet it and talk or sing to it.
  Animals tend to love when we sing to them or about them.
- Find out what the animal likes to eat and leave this out for it.
- Create a song, poem, or story for or about them. (I made up a
  sweet little song about crows one evening, and the next morning
  on my hike, there was a beautiful crow feather on the trail
  at my feet).
- Create a mask of its face or wear regalia representing it and engage
  in a ceremony with these items.
- Learn more about the nuances of how it adapts and survives in its

environment. If it happens to be your animal coessence, you probably share similar survival traits.

◄ Dance with your animal, and let it dance through you.

◄ Ask the animal to help you in areas it is particularly skilled at. For example, eagles are known for their bravery and courage. If this is an area you need help in, invite them into your life, and thank them for helping you with this challenge.

CATHY STRENGTHENS HER ENERGY LINES OF COMMUNICATION

Cathy came to me for soul retrieval and *sobaderismo* (shamanic body healing) sessions after a traumatic car accident. An eighteen-wheeler had hit her small Prius while she was driving on the freeway. It had slammed her car up along the center divider, completely totaling it and leaving her in shock. Cathy shared with me her frustration about the driver of the eighteen-wheeler lying to the police and claiming that she had been speeding. As a result, the insurance company was only offering her $5,000 to settle her claim, despite the shock she experienced, the few weeks of work she missed, and the severe back pain she was still experiencing. She also shared with me that she had been having nightly dreams of white owls. She was very worried about this since in Armenian culture, owls convey negative connotations or omens of death.

After our platica and tuning in to her energy field in a trance journey, I shared with her some of the understandings of owls in Mesoamerican culture and what I sensed. I reassured with her that owls are incredibly magical, wise, and courageous birds. They come into our lives to show us where we are stagnant and can inspire us to shift out of this stagnancy. So while owls were indeed associated with the Underworld in ancient Mesoamerica, the Underworld is associated with transformative medicine as well as death.

I encouraged Cathy to connect with the owl's courage, wisdom, and magic to help her to reveal that the driver of the eighteen-wheeler had lied. I advised her to smudge* her house to cleanse it of any negative energy and then create space for an altar in a special place in the house. I told her to then go online to obtain a picture of the type of owl that she was seeing in her dream. I also advised her to write a love letter to the owl, asking for its aid in being courageous and wise and working its magic to reveal the truth. She would place this love letter on a special shawl with her favorite crystals and leave it outside overnight on the next full moon to call on the energy of completion and closure and use it to charge the items and circumstances. The next morning she would place the shawl, crystals, feather, and picture of the owl on a small table in the space she had reserved, creating an altar for the owl. Because Cathy had been referred to me by a trusted friend who swore I had helped change her life and marriage for the better, she was open to what I was proposing.

Before the accident, Cathy had spent her free time engaging in activities she felt were meaningless, which pretty much involved watching television and eating junk food and whatever she could place into the microwave; she felt too tired after work to do anything else. After the accident, she continued to engage in the same meaningless activities, but since she was also experiencing intense pain in her mid- to lower back, she became severely depressed as well. She was in the Underworld in the sense that she was being tested to shift her prior old habits of approaching life as a meaningless rinse-and-repeat cycle.

Once she began seeing me, she started engaging in five to ten minutes of solar breathwork exercises each day to garner soul energy from the sun. (I relay many of these simple energy-bolstering exercises in *Sacred Energies of the Sun and Moon*.) She also began taking restorative yoga classes, which not only helped her with her back pain but also

---

*Smudging involves burning a dry bundle of herbs and allowing the smoke to be diffused throughout the space you would like to cleanse.

squelched her need to seek instant gratification from food, and she was able to lose weight. She started having more energy all around and was actually smiling and laughing considerably more in our sessions.

After a couple of months, she came to me feeling slightly anxious because the insurance company had hired an attorney and scheduled her deposition. Interestingly, the evening she received the deposition notice, she was at the ATM pulling out money, when a white owl flew over her. She said that although this may have previously created more anxiety within her, it seemed to calm her down this time. For that session, we connected with the spirit of the owl and requested its magic, courage, and wisdom in helping to resolve this claim in an ideal way. After the session, I suggested that Cathy buy a seven-day saint candle, light it, and place it on top of her petition on her small owl altar.

After her deposition a couple of weeks later, I received an email from her proclaiming victory and news that her case was settling for $35,000. She came in to see me a week later and was absolutely elated. She said her deposition had gone very well but that something very odd had happened on her way to it. She was on the 110 freeway in downtown Los Angeles about to get on the 10 West freeway, when she saw a white owl fly over her. Although she knew that owls are primarily nocturnal, she insisted that she had seen a beautiful large white owl fly over her as she was driving during the day. She felt a sense of calm and knew at the essence of her being that everything was going to work out in her favor.

Cathy was very pleased with the $35,000 offer but most importantly she was incredibly happy with the new routine she had integrated in her life. She had lost fifteen pounds and was in the best shape she had been in for a very long time. She was managing any lingering pain by going to yoga at least four times during the work week and sometimes once on the weekend. She was cooking for herself and eating more fresh green salads. She was also meditating regularly and developing her own spiritual practice, which, of course, included honoring and working with animal medicine.

PART TWO

Animal Allies A to Z

*Ancient Mesoamerican
Animal Mythologies,
Spiritual and
Shapeshifting Medicine,
and Symbolism*

◨ ◨ ◨

Part two begins with discussing some of the ancient Mesoamerican associations, mythologies, and ceremonies of each animal to keep these sacred traditions and beliefs flourishing within our hearts and minds and also to provide greater insight as to their sacred meanings and ways to communicate with them. Thereafter, I disclose the nonordinary realm(s) they were associated with, as they can be more readily accessed through their nonordinary realm and the medicine of these realms can also be accessed through them. To access an animal and medicine of the Upperworld refer to pages 18 to 26; to access an animal and medicine of the Middleworld refer to pages 27 to 32; and to access an animal and medicine of the Underworld refer to pages 32 to 37.

Next, I discuss the shapeshifting medicine each animal provides. Should you decide to obtain these medicines by shapeshifting into them via etheric or astral shifting practices, refer to pages 51 to 57. Although joining, physical, and bilocation are an option, these latter types of shifting practices are usually for more advanced shifters that have a high degree of balanced animating soul energies. Finally, I cover the symbolic meanings of these animals, should you see them in your dreams, physically, in meditation, or in journey. Read each symbolic meaning and see which one(s) give you an energy surge to determine the message the animal has for you. Refer to pages 70 to 71 to learn how to develop tuning into and assessing intuitive energy surges.

⚙ American Bittern ⚙

This large resilient waterbird typically resided in muddy marshes. It is a species of wading bird from the heron family. It was associated with all three nonordinary realms because it can fly, often remains hidden and camouflaged on the ground in bushes, is principally nocturnal, and eats mainly fish. Its sweet singing at nighttime signaled the coming of heavy rain, as well as an abundant amount of fish and other water life.[1]

Nonordinary Realm Associations: Upperworld, Middleworld, and Underworld

Spiritual and Shapeshifting Medicine: covertness, survival, courageous vocalizing, and resourcefulness

Symbolism Meanings

- State your truth and do so from a space of patience, compassion, and understanding.
- Make space for your choices in life by ensuring that your mental and emotional states correlate with them.
- Approach changes as opportunities for learning and growth, and something beautiful and prosperous will come of them.
- Stay hidden and unseen. There is someone or something you need to stay out of the line of fire from.

⚙ Ant ⚙

Ants in general were principally depicted as diligent and arduous workers. Larger ants, however, were thought of as dangerous and treacherous. Diego de Landa indicates that there were large ants whose venom was even more painful than that of a scorpion.[2]

In the Maya Popol Vuh, ants help the Hero Twins to pass their tests in the Razor House of the Underworld. They collect flower petals in four bowls for the Hero Twins.[3] Large ants were also associated with solar eclipses. Sixteenth-century missionary and Maya ethnographer

Diego López de Cogolludo indicates that large ants (*xibal*, in Yucatec Mayan) were known to attack and eat the sun.[4]

In the Legend of the Suns, Quetzalcoatl sees a red ant carrying a kernel of maize and asks where it found this food. The ant refuses to tell him. Quetzalcoatl shapeshifts into a black ant to find where they were storing the maize. Quetzalcoatl then takes some maize to Tamoanchan, a place of origin, to feed humans and give them strength.[5] Because of their ability to create tunnels under the earth, ants were associated with the Underworld.[6] Seeing an anthill inside a home signified restlessness and possibly negative energy being directed at the family that could lead to sickness.[7]

Nonordinary Realm Associations: Middleworld and Underworld

Spiritual and Shapeshifting Medicine: discipline, diligence, intuition, and, if a large ant, surprising fierceness

Symbolism Meanings

- ◄ It is time to get to work and be disciplined in your endeavors.
- ◄ Follow your intuition, and you will be rewarded and pleasantly surprised.
- ◄ Be open to working in community with a group of like-minded and like-hearted people. You will make more impactful strides in this way.
- ◄ Be discerning, and do not assume anything from merely looking at appearances.

❋ Armadillo ❋

In the artwork and mythology of Mesoamerica, the nine-banded armadillo predominates even though all twenty species of armadillo are found in the Americas. This is probably because the nine jointed plates around its midriff correspond to the nine levels of the Underworld. Their remarkably rapid and efficient digging capabilities link them to the Underworld as well. The cosmic number four of the cardinal spaces, completion, and grounding was also related to armadillos since they often bear quadruplets of the same sex.[8] In addition, armadillos were associated with music and dancing. On Classic Maya vases, they are depicted as drummers, likely due to their shell-like armored body that was used for drumming-related instruments, and in the Popol Vuh, the Hero Twins perform an armadillo dance in the Underworld. Trumpets were also made from their shells.[9]

Nonordinary Realm Associations: Middleworld and Underworld
Spiritual and Shapeshifting Medicine: determination, vigilance, carefulness, and selectivity
Symbolism Meanings
- Gift yourself with some time to dig deep within and reflect on where you have been, what you are grateful for, and what is next.
- There is a situation that you need to explore more deeply and thoroughly. There is something you are not seeing or understanding.
- Take some time to ground and clear your internal energy systems with music and movement; it is needed.
- Set clear boundaries, and hold true to them.

❀ Badger ❀

These short-legged omnivores were known by the Maya to be very strong, mischievous, and tenacious. Although badgers could be aggressive, they were known to be tamed and loved by women, which gave them Middleworld associations.[10] They are nocturnal animals and are excellent diggers with a great sense of smell and hearing. They typically live in extensive underground burrows, giving them a strong link to the Underworld.

Nonordinary Realm Associations: Middleworld and Underworld

Spiritual and Shapeshifting Medicine: persistence, insidiousness, clairaudience, and playfulness

Symbolism Meanings

◄ Do not let yourself become discouraged; be persistent and keep at it.

◄ Make some time to be playful and adventurous; your spirit needs it.

◄ Temper any assertiveness with a lighthearted and joyful spirit and demeanor.

◄ Sharpen your natural empathic tendencies into skills by being considerate of other people's feelings, while at the same time honoring your own and other people's boundaries.

☀ Barn Swallow ☀

Barn swallows are small waterbirds with pointed bills, short legs, and bright blue feathers. Although they are small, their call was known to be mighty and woke people up from their sleep.[11] For the K'iché', Maya, and Hopi, swallows were, and often still are, thought to be keen observers that acted as guides to help keep people safe in their journeys.[12]

Nonordinary Realm Associations: Upperworld, Middleworld, and Underworld

Spiritual and Shapeshifting Medicine: outspokenness, observation, forcefulness, and discernment

Symbolism Meanings

◄ Do not back down in articulating how you feel and what you need.

◂ You are being called to act as a mentor or teacher. Trust your skills and abilities in doing so.

◂ Assess the situation as a present, detached, and objective observer, and then take action.

◂ As someone's guide and mentor, let yourself be compassionate yet candid.

❀ Bat ❀

The two most predominant types of bats in Mesoamerican art and myth were the leaf-nosed bat and the vampire bat. Because a bat is nocturnal, navigates by sonar, and is known to reside in dark caves, it was strongly associated with the Underworld. It was also linked to both death and fertility, since it is a nocturnal pollinator.[13]

In Maya art, the bat's nocturnal nature was expressed by the *ak'bal* day sign, signifying night and power, which was often placed in or above their eyes or as an eyelid or brow.[14] In Classic Maya vases, they were often depicted with death symbols, crossed bones, or pulled-out eyes on their wings and scrolls like vegetation coming out of their mouths. The vampire bat often symbolized the ritual drawing of human blood.[15] In the Popol Vuh, the House of Bats was one of the treacherous nine levels of the Underworld that the Hero Twins had to pass before they were ultimately resurrected. The house was full of large bats, whose snouts were like blades and took off the head of one of the twins, Hunahpu.[16] The leaf-nosed bat was also seen as an Underworld deity, Zotz.[17]

In the Central Mexican Codex Borgia, the bat was depicted alongside maize and flowers and other animals associated with fertility and the rainy season, such as bees, butterflies, and hummingbirds (see plate 2).[18] Bats were also strongly associated with the principal Underworld deity, Mictlantecuhtli.[19] In the Codex Magliabechiano, a bat is born from the semen of the wind deity Quetzalcoatl and plays a part in the release of fragrant flowers. While lunar and earth deity Xochiquetzal is sleeping, a bat takes a bite of her vulva. When the gods wash the piece of her flesh, only malodorous flowers come forth. But when the bat takes the flesh to the Mictlantecuhtli, fragrant flowers emerge from the flesh.[20]

Nonordinary Realm Associations: Underworld
Spiritual and Shapeshifting Medicine: clairaudience, sociability, loyalty, and adaptability
Symbolism Meanings

- Make time and space to be sociable with people who share common interests.
- Allow yourself to grow, learn, and persevere from any challenging or turbulent periods in your life.
- There is someone who is close to you that needs you to stop and truly listen to them.
- While you are working on releasing patterns and ways of thinking that no longer serve you, simultaneously begin or continue to integrate positive new patterns and ways of being and thinking.

❀ Bee ❀

Diverse ethnohistorical and epigraphic sources clearly indicate that bees held and continue to hold a very privileged position in Mesoamerican culture.[21] Bees were thought of as divine beings or divinity itself and were strongly associated with abundance, happiness, and fertility.

Honeybees were domesticated by the ancient Maya and are still raised by the K'iché', particularly in the mountain villages surrounding Momostenango.[22] Stingless honeybees were important trade items. Bees were pictured principally in the Madrid Codex, where a giant bee inhabits a temple or house.[23] Pages 111a and 112b of the Madrid Codex show pictures of gods with brooms in their hands, which likely relate to apiculture, especially beehive cleaning. A modern-day beehive *limpia*, or spiritual cleansing, known as *santiguar* is performed to protect bees from dangerous epidemics and attacks from xulab ants. The *hmen* (curanderx) use brooms made of anointed leaves to clean the beehives as they recite prayers.[24]

In the month of Sotz, on the Maya solar calendar, the proprietors of beehives prepared themselves to celebrate their festival Tzec in the following month by fasting. For the Tzec festival, they honored the quadripartite deities associated with the cardinal directions, one of which was Jobnil, an eponymous deity associated with beehives. The offerings to Jobnil included small balls of incense, each painted with small "effigies of honey" or "drawings of honey." The purpose of this ceremony was to welcome in abundance. In the solar month of Mol, beekeepers made rounds to the beehives to make offerings, so that the gods would provide flowers for the bees.[25] In the Book of Chilam Balam of Chumayel, wild bees were also associated with a ritual to the four quarters of the world, reflecting their association with creation and divinity.[26]

Bees were also commonly found in the months associated with fertility and the rainy season in the Codex Borgia.[27] A hundred years after the conquest, apiculturists still used spells to find beehives. Some people believed bees to be the sacred energy and the divine priest from Tollan, a paradisal realm of flower fields.[28] It was said that to collect honey, it was imperative to be in a calm state of mind "because [the bees] feel like gods; because they provide men with what is necessary, and they do not like tribulations."[29]

Nonordinary Realm Associations: Upperworld and Middleworld
Spiritual and Shapeshifting Medicine: commitment, cooperation, personal power, and organization
Symbolism Meanings

◄ Be willing to work in a community of like-hearted and like-minded people; your efforts to work in a community will be substantially impactful.

◄ It is time to get organized, especially concerning your career and the abundance you can create from it.

◄ Engage in some honey-centered ceremonies to attract abundance, such as lathering yourself in honey after a good limpia and then showering off.

◄ Be mindful that the divine is in all things, including what may seem trivial and small.

❋ Black Skimmer ❋

The black skimmer is a small black waterbird that was known to fly high in the sky at night over the lagoons of Central Mexico. It warned of impending danger. Fishermen were careful to avoid capturing them, as it was believed that doing so would bring misfortune.[30]

Nonordinary Realm Associations: Upperworld, Middleworld, and Underworld

Spiritual and Shapeshifting Medicine: magic, intuition, prophecy, and freedom

Symbolism Meanings

◄ Be mindful of what you are trying to attain and the motives behind it. Stay humble, grounded, and balanced.

◄ Use your magic to pave your path and ensure that it is more graceful and ideal.

◄ There are people around you that may unintentionally or possibly intentionally be envious of you; make sure you do periodic limpias to cleanse yourself of those energies.

◄ Take time to do a ceremony with the moon or at one of the earth's bodies of water, and manifest what you choose.

❋ Butterfly ❋

Butterflies, along with flowers and precious birds, were dominant themes in the Upperworld Flower World paradise in ancient Mesoamerica. The Central Mexican people, going back to Teotihuacan, associated butterflies with ancestors.[31] In the Mexica's Nahui Ollin (four motion) rite, their feast to honor the sun, they offered incense to an image of the sun depicted as a butterfly in a golden circle emitting radiant beams and glowing lines.[32] They believed that four years after brave warriors died they would become birds, hummingbirds, or butterflies and spend the rest of eternity drinking nectar from flowers from the Upperworld paradisal flower realm and from flowers on earth.[33] The Codex Kingsborough depicts Xochiquetzal on a war shield as a swallowtail butterfly. Swallowtail butterflies are known for their aggressive behavior, appropriate for this warrior aspect of Xochiquetzal.[34] In the Codex Borgia they are associated with the fertile and rainy seasons of the year.[35]

While the association of butterflies with the floral paradise and the sacred essence energy held at the brow of the head was rather pervasive in ancient Mesoamerica, the ancient Maya generally did not associate their ancestors with butterflies. They typically depicted butterflies as bug-like insects, skeletal beings of death and darkness, instead of light and beauty.[36] A common symbolic element in the Maya codex-style vessels is the depiction of the head of the War Serpent, Waxaklaju'n Ubaah Kan, an ophidian of an igneous nature combining the attributes of a jaguar and a butterfly.[37] The Tzotziles of San Andres Larrainzar believe that some of the most fearsome naguals are insects, specifically the butterfly and the cricket.[38]

Nonordinary Realm Associations: Upperworld and Middleworld
Spiritual and Shapeshifting Medicine: rebirth, transformation, hope, and bravery
Symbolism Meanings

◄ Be hopeful; positive change is transpiring. Take some time to meditate in the sun, and let it grace you with sacred essence energy and energize you for this change.

◄ There are brave forces watching over you and ensuring graceful transitions for you.

◄ Let yourself gracefully flow with a rebirth and transformation.

◄ It is time to spread your wings and explore new ventures. How will you know whether you like something unless you try it?

❋ Caiman (Alligator and Crocodile) ❋

While alligators, crocodiles, and caimans are distinct from one another, they are close relatives and share similar physical attributes, as well as analogous mythological symbolism. They were associated with both celestial and terrestrial regenerative aspects and portals to cosmic and nonordinary realms and were often conflated with trees, elements, and deer.

For the Maya, their backs were a metaphor of the earth's surface, wherein each leg was a corner of the earth.[39] The creator deity, Itzamna (Deity D), is often portrayed coming out of a bicephalic caiman.[40] When they were depicted floating on water, they symbolized the earth above the Underworld.[41] According to the Books of Chilam Balam from Tizimin, Mani, and Chumayel, to avoid complete annihilation after a flood and bringing down the skies, the gods dismember a caiman, and parts of its body become the new surface of the earth.[42] In the Dresden Codex, the Starry Deer Caiman is deliberately sacrificed to destroy the world and revive it.[43]

Maya rulers were often represented as crocodile trees to signify regenerative abilities and skills in accessing nonordinary realms. In Classic period Copan, in the lower portion of the east side of Stela C (stone slabs of artwork), the ruler 18 Rabbit is portrayed in the form of a crocodile tree emerging from a mountain.[44] Crocodile ceiba trees were also understood to be portals between the world and the nonordinary realms.[45]

In the Central Mexican *History of Mexico*, a crocodile is split into two halves, and four gods get in between them to serve as cardinal spaces and a tripartite cosmovision of the nonordinary realms. The dismembered body of the crocodile forms the world.[46] In many instances of the Codex Borgia, Tonacatecuhtli, an aged deity associated with earth and the heavens, birth, creation, fire, and maize, wears the spiny skin of the caiman.[47] On pages 39 and 40 of the codex, the open mouth of the earth crocodile signals an entrance into the earth, likely the Underworld, that Stripe Eye and Xochipilli enter (see plate 3).[48] Caiman, or alligator, (Ce Cipactli) was the first day sign of the Mexica's tonalpohualli (divinatory calendar) and was associated with the east. Those born under this day sign were said to be fortunate, hard workers, never wasteful, and good with finances.[49]

It was also considered great fortune if someone saw a crocodile, alligator, or caiman. When people living on the river plains saw a crocodile, alligator, or caiman, they would jump on its neck and let themselves go downstream until they arrived at their settlement or hut.[50]

Nonordinary Realm Associations: Upperworld, Middleworld, and Underworld

Spiritual and Shapeshifting Medicine: assertiveness, patience, cunning, and instinctual power

Symbolism Meanings

◄ You already have the tools to create something new and fortuitous. Slow down and reconsider your gifts and talents. You already have everything you need.

◄ Assert your personal boundaries and know that by doing so you are also claiming space for you to create and recreate yourself.

◄ A new beginning is on the horizon, so prepare yourself and make it worthwhile.

◄ Connect with your ancestors, whether it be through a simple prayer or a more elaborate ceremony. They have medicine that can greatly serve you at this time in your life.

❀ Catfish (Fish) ❀

Catfish and fish in general were metaphors for water and were connected to the moon, likely because the moon controls the tides and all bodies of water.[51] Catfish are bottom-feeders and recycle waste into food that is eaten by other marine life. The barbell at the side of their mouth is loaded with tiny taste buds and olfactory sensors to help them smell and sense food.

The Maya sun deity, Deity G, was often depicted with a tendril or catfish barbell on the corner of his mouth, possibly signaling his ability to recycle mundane energies into precious soul animating energy.[52] Chaac Deity B, the Maya rain deity, was another god associated with fish in general. The Classic period Palenque Creation Tablet describes Chaac as a fisherman, and the late Preclassic Izapa Stela 1 reveals fishing to be a rainmaking act. The classic fish-in-hand glyph is read *tsak*, meaning "to fish and conjure." On early Classic stelae from Tikal, Caracol, and Calakmul, rulers wear a stylized fish on their wrists and ankles while holding a ceremonial bar used for conjuring gods and ancestors.[53]

In the Popol Vuh and various twin-related vase imagery, after the Hero Twins are ground up and thrown into the river, they are transformed into catfish and then later resurrected back into their human form, or they are eaten by catfish that are later swallowed by waterbirds, who then give new human life to the Hero Twins.[54] The Maya undoubtedly understood the bottom-feeding behavior of catfish as having the ability to recycle detritus and waste into precious energy, even new life.[55]

In Central Mexico, fish had transformative connotations, particularly as people who had been transformed into fish in a previous world. In the Fourth Sun of the Legend of the Suns, a great flood destroyed the world, and its people are transformed into fish.[56] In the South Ballcourt panels of Late Classic El Tajin, Panels 5 and 6 depict scenes similar to sequences in the Legend of the Suns in which Quetzalcoatl steals bones from the Underworld to create humankind and takes maize from the mountain of sustenance. However, rather than Quetzalcoatl, Tlaloc, the Central Mexican rain deity, is the central protagonist who on Panel 5 appears to disperse penile blood onto primordial fish-men from an earlier creation episode.[57]

Nonordinary Realm Associations: Underworld

Spiritual and Shapeshifting Medicine: transfiguration, evolution, adaptability, and intuition

Symbolism Meanings

◄ Refrain from simply throwing out old ideas; reenvision them and give them new life.

◄ Allow your intuitive senses to guide you more in life; it will help to make your life more graceful.

◄ Continue to develop your emotional and intuitive intelligence. These gifts and skills will be invaluable in the leadership roles that are opening up for you.

◄ Learn the lessons from difficult circumstances and people before simply moving on.

❂ Centipede ❂

The centipede was deeply associated with death and the Underworld, as well as the cycle of death and rebirth. By day, centipedes hide under stones or logs on the ground, beneath loose bark, in rotting wood, in caves, and other similar subterranean regions of darkness.[58] Both the Maya sun deity and an Underworld deity often fashioned headdresses with centipedes.[59] Central Mexican lunar-related deities, Xochiquetzal and Tlazolteotl in Postclassic codices were associated with centipedes.[60]

Centipedes were connected to the newly born sun as it emerged daily out of the Underworld. At nighttime when the sun set, the sun deity was believed to shapeshift into a jaguar at night and roam the Underworld, and at the same time the aspect of the sun deity that did not become a jaguar was carried by a centipede through the Underworld. The centipede eventually released the sun at dawn in the east.[61]

Skeletal centipede maws served as places of cosmic emergence and portals. The sarcophagus lid of ruler K'inich Janaab' Pakal I in Classic period Palenque depicts his departure from the Underworld via the maws of a centipede. The resurrected ruler rises up along a world tree, which acts as an axis mundi, or portal, that transfers his body to a flowery realm in the Upperworld.[62] The "vision serpent" of Lintels 13 and 14 of Classic period site Yaxchilan are also likely a centipede as noted by the segmented body with multiple appendages and the shape of the frontal teeth. In both lintels, the future king is the character who emerges as a newborn from the maw of a centipede, possibly Lady Chak-Skull's way, winding around her waist, "an elaborate visual metaphor of birth."[63]

A late Maya Classic stucco vessel depicts a singing musician with rattles in the centipede mouth, a scene relating to the ritual importance of utilizing music to communicate with and conjure the deceased and the centipede being a conduit into this realm.[64] The Dumbarton Oaks vessel K4340 shows a male and female sitting in the jaws of a centipede snake that represents a cave mouth that acts as a portal.

The Central Mexican peoples gathered poisonous insects and reptiles, such as spiders, scorpions, centipedes, lizards, and vipers; burned them in a brazier temple; and included the ashes in other plant mixtures such as tobacco and morning glory, as well as in ointments for their bodies, sacred beverages to offer to their deities, and medicines to cure the sick and little children.[65] It is possible that the quinoline alkaloid within the venom of centipedes acted as a stimulant in these mixtures.

Nonordinary Realm Associations: Underworld

Spiritual and Shapeshifting Medicine: spiritual awakening, revival, portentousness, and energy

Symbolism Meanings

- It is time to go deeper on your spiritual path and journey. Take time and space to invest in yourself and something that you feel is intuitively calling you.
- Seek out and try different spiritual adventures and experiences; refrain from allowing yourself to become stagnant.
- Approach matters with balance and spiritual discernment.
- Let yourself be a guide and mentor for those around you going

through difficult times, while establishing loving and healthy boundaries.

☀ Coati ☀

The coati, a lowlands raccoon-like animal with a prominently pointed nose and long tail, was known as an intelligent animal that was associated with the feminine aspect of divine creation by many Maya. Coatis were prominent in agricultural and fertility rites, likely due to their ability to bear many babies and their voracious appetite.[66] One of the K'iché' creator deities, Gucumatz, was identified as a coati in addition to other agricultural names.[67] In the Popol Vuh, Xmucane, the feminine aspect of the creator couple, is a coati, which is also another name or title for the female creator goddess.[68]

Nonordinary Realm Associations: Middleworld and Underworld

Spiritual and Shapeshifting Medicine: intelligence, generosity, exuberance, and design

Symbolism Meanings

◄ Be confident in your ability to influence and shape your path. You are the master of your destiny.

◄ Incorporate more compassion and tolerance in your approach with new people and circumstances.

◄ Engage in acts of goodwill, generosity, and kindness. Along with revitalizing and helping others, you will also revitalize your soul and spirit.

◄ Reach out to your blood or spiritual family for guidance and support, and let them do the same for you. Lovingly build and grow your support systems.

☀ Cormorant ☀

The cormorant bird is known for being able to dive deep in water, about 147 feet. Their deep-diving abilities likely gave them transformative and shapeshifting connotations, and they were often conflated with other waterbirds in iconographic representations. They also tended to appear in conjunction with the rebirth of the Maya maize deity, who is commonly associated with cyclical change and transformation, which suggests that cormorants also had similar associations.[69] Their special shapeshifting shamanic-related correlations also made them fitting to aid rulers. In Tikal, at the Central Acropolis, Structure 5D-52 Lintel 2 from the Classic period shows a ruler being attended by a dwarf and cormorants.

Nonordinary Realm Associations: Upperworld, Middleworld, and Underworld

Spiritual and Shapeshifting Medicine: transformation, freedom, spontaneity, and independence

Symbolism Meanings

◄ Stop limiting yourself; it is time to let yourself soar.

◄ Dive deep and reflect on what brings you happiness and what feels right for you; let this pave your path.

◄ Take the lead in believing in what you can do and go for it.

◄ You are a natural curanderx-shaman; develop these gifts and abilities.

☀ Coyote ☀

The K'iché' believed the coyote to be a cunning nocturnal animal that discovered and dug up hidden or secret things.[70] The coyote's high predatorial skills also granted it a valued space in the creator echelon; it was one of the first sons of the creator couple, Xmucane and Xpiyacoc, in the Popol Vuh.[71]

The Central Mexican peoples also viewed the coyote as being diabolical but at the same time grateful and appreciative. Sahagún was told of a story of a warrior who had saved a coyote from a serpent. Two hours after being rescued, the coyote brought the warrior two turkey cocks and pushed them with his muzzle as if to say, take them.[72] One of their creator deities, Tezcatlipoca, was known to shapeshift into a coyote.[73] Nobles born on Ce Ehecatl were also able to shapeshift into this esteemed predator.[74]

The coyote, like the jaguar and eagle, was a patron of Mexica elite warriors and was associated with one of the primary military orders. Their military clothing bore the skins of pumas, coyotes, wildcats, jaguars, and eagles, and their head coverings included jaguars and coyotes.[75]

One of the Central Mexican deities, Huehuecoyotl (old coyote), was a coyote deity linked with song, dance, pleasure, deceit, and sexuality.[76] The Codex Borbonicus and Codex Tonalamatl Aubin emphasize his musical proclivities (see plate 4), and the Codex Borgia and Codex Vaticanus focus on his dancing. In most examples, Huehuecoyotl wears a necklace of pointed shells and a distinctive shell pendant of a pointed oval, costuming usually associated with gods of feasting and dancing.[77]

Nonordinary Realm Associations: Underworld

Spiritual and Shapeshifting Medicine: musical talent, charisma, sensuality, and shrewdness

Symbolism Meanings

- ◄ Let yourself shake off any unwanted energies and tap into the sacred energies all around you with ecstatic dancing.
- ◄ Explore energetic tantric teachings and courses to better understand and work with sensual-sexual energies.
- ◄ You are naturally clairaudient. Develop this gift by learning to hear the energy of what is being said and trust your intuition.

◄ Go after what you desire with an open mind and heart. It may not be quite what you pictured, but it will be better than you imagined.

❀ Crow ❀

Crows were known for being able to spot precious items, particularly corn. The crow, along with the mountain cat, coyote, and small parrot, were the intelligent animals that brought the maize that was used to make the human race.[78] In the codices, blackbirds, including crows, were correlated with precarious omens and were depicted attacking maize.[79] Their love of corn, which is strongly associated with the cyclical aspects of the Middleworld and the earth's bounty, connects them to the Middleworld, while their ability to fly links them to the Upperworld.

I personally love crows and have been amazed by their loyalty. On one occasion, a crow committed a kamikaze attack on the window of a junior partner at a law firm when he began laughing uncontrollably at a horrible misfortune that had befallen me. In another instance, I had two crows blocking my way as I was going into a law firm for an interview. Although the crows were not rude, they did not get out of my way until I came within a few inches of them, and one of them left some kind of large kernel in front of me. The interview went very well, and they wanted me to start immediately. But I knew the crows had definitely given me a warning, and I did not take it lightly. When I got home from the interview, I looked up the senior attorney on the California State Bar portal and found out that he had been disciplined twice. I did some more research on the internet and found out that this law firm had been implicated in real estate fraud. I have found crows to be incredibly intelligent and very easy to communicate with.

Nonordinary Realm Associations: Upperworld and Middleworld
Spiritual and Shapeshifting Medicine: magic, adaptability, loyalty, and craftiness
Symbolism Meanings

◄ You are being divinely cared for and guided; pay attention and have faith.

- ◄ It is time to engage in a magical rite or two, alongside your practical efforts in manifesting what you choose.
- ◄ Let go of your fear of change and learn to adapt and thrive in different environments. Great fortune will unfold in unexpected ways.
- ◄ Accept support and help from friends and loved ones; do not try to do everything on your own.

❂ Curve-Billed Thrasher ❂

The curve-billed thrasher bird was loved and domesticated by the Central Mexicans for its beautiful singing. It has long, strong, skinny legs and a slender curved bill, and its dark ash color[80] acts as camouflage in its typical desert and canyon surroundings.

Nonordinary Realm Associations: Upperworld and Middleworld
Spiritual and Shapeshifting Medicine: innocence, lightheartedness, wisdom, and imperceptibility
Symbolism Meanings
- ◄ You are taking yourself and life, in general, way too seriously. Set aside some time to color, be silly, or simply play and be playful.
- ◄ When you speak your truth, do so with directness and sweetness at the same time. It will have a better chance of being understood and better received.
- ◄ Infuse more creativity in your business ventures. Do not fall into stagnant patterns and habits—shake it up a bit.
- ◄ Your energetic presence is hard to ignore. Be sure that you know how to cloak it when necessary.

❂ Deer ❂

The nimble speed and grace of the deer made it a favorable symbol of rulership and stellar metaphors. Deer often played recurring roles in creation myths[81] and were linked with the earth's fertility and prevalent in hunting and fertility rites.[82] The white deer was said to be a ruler among other deer.[83]

In Maya creation myths, the Starry Deer Crocodile, a celestial hybrid of a deer and a crocodile, is a consistent actor in creation myths and the formation of the cosmos. The decapitation of the Starry Deer Crocodile causes the destruction of the prior world through a succession of fire and floods but then also leads to the renewal of this world.[84] The major iconographic features of House E at Classic period Palenque is the Two-Headed Celestial Dragon, or Starry Deer Crocodile, a nocturnal manifestation of the Celestial Monster that symbolizes the Milky Way, an iconographic portal.[85] In the Popol Vuh, deer, along with birds, jaguars, and serpents—forest mountain animals—were among the first beings created to inhabit the earth. But because the animals were unable to speak properly and worship the gods, the creators decided that they would not be given dominion over the earth; instead they would remain in the wild and be food for people.[86]

Deer were also associated with the sun and its renewal. The celestial deer served as a mode of transport for the sun during the dry season of the year.[87] Deer were also often depicted as seducing the moon, a likely allusion to the phases of the moon and personifications of astronomical phenomena.[88]

On Classic Maya vases, deer are often accompanied by death symbols, which may allude to transformation rather than simply death. These images appear to depict the Headband Gods—paired manifestations of Deity S who tried to revive their dead father but instead of their father coming back as human, he was transformed into a deer.[89]

On page 33 of the Central Mexican Codex Borgia there is a description of a white cord, likely the ecliptic, that descends from a temple and has attached to it a series of heavenly and religious elements, including the deer as the sun (see plate 7).[90] In the tonalpohualli, the Mexica's divinatory calendar, the deer (*mazatl*) was the seventh day sign and was associated with the west. Those born under this sign were believed to be fortunate and successful. They were typically fond of the woods and hunting and liked to travel.[91] If they were born under Ce Mazatl (one deer), however, they were timid, weak spirited, and fainthearted.[92]

Nonordinary Realm Associations: Upperworld, Middleworld, and Underworld

Spiritual and Shapeshifting Medicine: grace, bounty, transformation, and enlivenment

Symbolism Meanings

◄ Be kind and gentle with yourself; you deserve it and are worth it.

◄ The time is ripe for seeking out new experiences and adventures.

◄ Move away from toxic people and circumstances, and move toward what is healthy and loving for you.

◄ Take the time to soak in all the gifts and lessons from unexpected outcomes and reflect on what the universe is mirroring to you.

✸ Dog ✸

Dogs were known to be playful, happy, and loyal companions.[93] They were believed to help the deceased cross a river and guided them through the Underworld.[94] Classic Maya vases, such as Kerr Vase 594, depict a deceased individual being accompanied by a dog. The vases also suggest that a dog may have been an animal coessence or power animal of the death deity, Deity A. Dogs were also known for their tracking abilities and helped hunters trap quail and deer. They were domesticated by the Maya as early as 3000 BCE and were typically maintained in shared courtyards.[95]

In the Legend of the Suns, immediately before a cataclysmic flood in the period of the Fourth Sun, the deity Tezcatlipoca instructed a couple, Tata and Nene, to save themselves in a hollowed-out giant cypress. He told them to eat only one maize kernel each. When they finally came out, they lit a fire and cooked a fish. Because of their disobedience, Tezcatlipoca became angry, cut off their heads, stuck them on their rumps, and turned them into dogs.[96] The creation of the small hairless dog may have been a hybridized dog, the Xoloitzcuintli, who as a puppy was dipped in a turpentine unguent so its hair would fall out.[97]

The Central Mexican peoples also buried tawny colored dogs with their deceased, as it was believed that only these colored dogs could transport the deceased to the Underworld.[98] Other instances relay that a little dog was cremated with the deceased.[99] Dog (*itzcuintli*) was the tenth day sign of the Mexica's tonalpohualli and was associated with the north. Those born on that day were said to be courageous, generous, and likely to ascend in the world, overflowing with abundance.[100] Nahualli commoners born on Ce Ehecatl could shapeshift into dogs, as well as turkeys or weasels.[101]

Another story in the Legend of the Suns was about the creation of humans that also tells of the animal coessence of Quetzalcoatl, Xolotl, a canine deity. Xolotl, the god of twins and deformities, was a skeletal dog-faced or dog-bodied god often depicted with torn ears.[102] Quetzalcoatl is also identified with twins; *coatl* means snake and twins.[103] In the legend, Quetzalcoatl went to the Underworld to recover the bones of the humans from the previous world. After doing so, Quetzalcoatl ran off with the bones but was pursued by Mictlantecuhtli's messengers and fell into a ditch. Xolotl came to the rescue, and Quetzalcoatl was able to take the bones to Tamoanchan, a place of origin, where the first humans were created.[104]

Xolotl is able to enter and exit the Underworld and consequently is able to guide the sun along its eastward journey through the Underworld. Every day, Xolotl helps the sun leave the Underworld and be reborn each morning.[105] On page 37 of the Codex Borgia, Xolotl is also depicted carrying a fire serpent into the Underworld, indicating the end of drought.[106]

Nonordinary Realm Associations: Middleworld and Underworld
Spiritual and Shapeshifting Medicine: loyalty, bravery, resourcefulness, and keen tracking

Symbolism Meanings

- ◄ Show your appreciation to those who have been loyal and appreciative of you.
- ◄ In times of change and ambiguity, have faith; you are always being divinely guided.
- ◄ Trust your intuition and sense of knowing, especially when you sense that things are not as they appear.
- ◄ Do not forget to let yourself be amused, in awe and gratitude for the simple things in life.

❂ Dove ❂

Doves were known to help strengthen trust and love in relationships. The partner they first mate with is the partner they stay with for life. When either of them dies, the other is known to cry and watch over their deceased partner by visiting the place where they died. The Central Mexicans believed that eating a dove's cooked flesh would help jealous partners forget their jealousy, strengthening the bonds in relationships.[114]

Nonordinary Realm Associations: Upperworld
Spiritual and Shapeshifting Medicine: devotion, faithfulness, love, and peace
Symbolism Meanings

- ◄ Reflect on the need to forgive anyone you feel may have wronged you, and release any heaviness weighing on your heart and soul.
- ◄ Be gentle with yourself, and engage in activities that emulate self-love and self-care.
- ◄ Find new ways of expressing your love and appreciation to the special people in your life; you will in turn be open to receiving more love.
- ◄ Peace, understanding, and forgiveness are on the horizon in a prior relationship where there was a falling out.

☀ Dragon ☀

It was common for Mesoamerican artists to combine different animal species to render mythical dragon-like creatures that could have the attributes of centipedes, snakes, crocodiles, and possibly other animals, such as sharks and lizards.[107] For the Maya, the dragon-crocodile represented primordial aquatic chaos that gave rise to the cosmos. It also symbolized creation and destruction, life and death, water, air, the earth, vegetation, and the tripartite vertical division of the world.[108] In K'iché' cosmogony, primordial water is a dragon.[109]

The bearded dragon was a conduit for conjuring gods and ancestors.[110] It was a creature of breath and wind and frequently rose out of burning bowls as swirling currents or was exhaled out of the mouths of zoomorphic mountains.[111] The Two-Headed Celestial Dragon, also known as the Cosmic Monster or Starry Deer Crocodile, personified the rainbow, ecliptic, or Milky Way and was a carrier of rain. It was a being through which transformation took place in the nonordinary realms.[112] The Maya day sign *cauac* in their divinatory calendar is associated with storms, thunder, and rain. It was the day of the celestial dragons that sent the rain and storms.[113]

Nonordinary Realm Associations: Upperworld, Middleworld, and Underworld

Spiritual and Shapeshifting Medicine: enigma, metamorphosis, creation, and restoration

Symbolism Meanings
- ◄ Continue to develop your imagination and connect deeper to your unconscious mind; there is something fantastic waiting to be uncovered.
- ◄ Connect with an ideal childlike innocence and purity, and allow these qualities to rejuvenate you.
- ◄ There is a heightened metamorphosis of consciousness and awareness within you taking place. Do not be weighed down by it; soar with it.

◄ Make time to engage in breathwork exercises, and let them purify and revitalize you.

۞ Dragonfly ۞

Dragonflies were allies of the sun and hummingbirds and in Central Mexico were associated with an abundant paradisal realm, Tlalocan (place of Tlaloc, the rain deity). In Maya mythologies involving an illicit affair between the sun and moon (or a maiden that would later become the moon), dragonflies helped the sun resurrect the moon. The earliest known recorded story was documented by Pablo Wirsig in 1909* and tells of a young moon maiden who was a weaver and lived with her father. Trying to impress her, the sun first posed as a hunter, carrying a stuffed deerskin, but the trick failed when he slid on the maize-cooking water that she threw on his path, following her father's advice. The sun then disguised himself as a hummingbird. Attracted by the beautiful bird, the girl asked her father to capture it for her. She first put it in a gourd, but it became restless, so she placed it inside her blouse. She went to bed with it on her chest. At midnight, the hummingbird shape-shifted into a man, and he and the moon maiden escaped. The father, angered by the deception, asked for help from his relative, lightning, who struck them with his axe as they reached a lake. The sun escaped by hiding inside a turtle carapace. The moon hid inside an armadillo's armor, but it broke, and lightning killed her, spilling her blood in the

*The story was narrated by Juan Caal and later published by Quirin Diesseldorff (1966–1967) and Estrada Monroy (1990).

water. With the help of dragonflies, the sun recovered the blood and placed it in thirteen jars.

When the sun later opened the jars, he found that the first twelve contained all kinds of serpents, lizards, biting insects, spiders, scorpions, centipedes, and caterpillars. The sun then asked a woodcutter to throw the jars in the lake. But the woodcutter was curious and opened them, letting the vermin out. The moon appeared in all her beauty from the thirteenth jar. Thereafter the sun and moon rose to the sky.[115]

The Classic Central Mexican mural of Tlalocan in the Tepantitla compound depicts dragonflies and butterflies in the paradisal realm, Tlalocan. There are small human figurines bathing and frolicking in the water, resting, cutting flowers, eating, singing, dancing, and playing.[116] Tlalocan was an earthly paradise of unending abundant vegetation. Those who died from phenomena associated with water, such as lightning, drowning, and waterborne diseases, went to Tlalocan.[117]

Nonordinary Realm Associations: Upperworld and Middleworld
Spiritual and Shapeshifting Medicine: enthusiasm, playfulness, inspiration, and good fortune
Symbolism Meanings
- ◄ Positive new beginnings are opening up for you; have faith.
- ◄ You are taking life way too seriously; take a step back and make time to play and rejoice.
- ◄ The fairies and other elementals are looking out for you; take some time to connect with them.
- ◄ Great fortune is coming your way; rejoice.

❀ Duck ❀

Ducks were associated with entrances to the Underworld, fertility, rebirth, wind, and a vitalizing force of life, breath.[118] The number of eggs a duck can lay in a single brood, or clutch, can be as many as twenty, which is likely why they were associated with fertility.

A duck-billed anthropomorphic being that is likely ancestral to the Late Postclassic Ehecatl-Quetzalcoatl is among the oldest deities in Mesoamerica. An anthropomorphic duck-billed being appears in a late Classic Maya vessel depicting a seated figure with a long bill decorated with T-shaped *ik'* (wind or breath) symbols on its arm and lower back.[119]

In the Late Postclassic period, the anthropomorphic duck-billed being appears as deity, Ehecatl-Quetzalcoatl often fashioning a spire out of a conch shell, a cut-conch ornament (*ehecailacocozcatl*). In his guise as a wind deity, Ehecatl-Quetzalcoatl was a life-giving aspect of wind. He was the road sweeper of the Tlaloc rain gods, the wind that brings the rain clouds. He was believed to have created heaven and earth and was associated with fertility, life, and water.[120]

During the sixth-month celebration of the Central Mexico rain deity, Tlaloc, curanderx would enter the lake and mimic the splashing and sounds of ducks, herons, and gulls, celebrating their current rainy season. The Central Mexicans also buried the deceased with Colima duck effigies. These ducks may have acted as spiritual guardians with implications of fertility and rebirth.[121]

Nonordinary Realm Associations: Middleworld and Underworld
Spiritual and Shapeshifting Medicine: zeal, rejuvenation, emotional balance, and fertility
Symbolism Meanings

◄ Take the time to clear yourself from others' emotions by engaging in limpias or breathwork to release energies or emotions that are not yours.

◄ Kundalini breathwork is a great investment for your mind, body, and spirit.

◄ It is a time of fertility and creation; reflect on what you are focusing on and would love to create in your life.

◄ Go within, to your underworld, and discern whether the emotions you are carrying are yours or belong to others. If they belong to others, set the intention to release them. If they are yours, be gentle and explore them.

❂ Eagle ❂

Eagles were identified with rulers, warriors, and the sun at its zenith, the period when it was believed to be at its strongest and gave its greatest degree of animating soul energies.[122] Tecun Uman, one of the last rulers of the K'iché' Maya in Guatemala, was said to have been able to shapeshift into a quetzal and an eagle. Before the arrival of the Spaniards, Tecun reportedly flew up into the sky as a quetzal. But afterward he took on a larger form, possibly an eagle, while defending his people against the Spanish invasion in 1524.[123] The Classic murals of Structure A at Cacaxtla depict Maya warriors dressed in eagle regalia standing on a plumed and bearded serpent.[124]

For the Central Mexicans, especially the Mexica, eagles served as their most fundamental emblems for the sun's disk and path. The paramount solar deity in Postclassic Mesoamerica was the sun deity, Tonatiuh, who is often portrayed wearing eagle feathers and seated within or surrounded by a large solar disk.[125] The Mexica's most exalted warriors were identified with the House of Eagles and House of Jaguars.[126] The eagle's fearlessness allowed it to gaze into the face of the sun.[127] In one of their creation mythologies, the Legend of the Suns, after Nanahuatzin threw himself into the fiery hearth and many other animals unsuccessfully attempted to pull him out of it, the eagle went in and was able to carry him out of the fire. Nanahuatzin rose up to become the sun, Tonatiuh.[128] The eagle (*quauhtli*) was the fifteenth day sign of the Mexica's tonalpohualli and

was associated with the west. Although those born under this day sign would likely be brave, there was also a likelihood that they would be vain and covet their neighbor's wealth.[129]

Nonordinary Realm Associations: Upperworld and Middleworld
Spiritual and Shapeshifting Medicine: courage, fearlessness, wisdom, and cleverness
Symbolism Meanings

◄ Take a step back and watch everything from afar. Once you have fully assessed the situation, move forward.

◄ Refrain from allowing perceived limitations to prevent you from soaring and living your best life.

◄ Merge your intuitive and practical skills, and put your goals into action one step at a time.

◄ Do not wait for permission to gain your freedom; claim it as yours, without question.

❀ Earthworm ❀

Earthworms increase the amount of air and water in the soil and can sense sunlight through their skin. They feed on the waste of animals and plants and break it down to a beneficial fertilizer. This ability to enhance the quality of soil likely leads earthworms to play a vital role in helping Quetzalcoatl pass his tests in the Central Mexican creation story, the Legend of the Suns. Mictlantecuhtli required Quetzalcoatl to blow music from a solid conch shell before he would agree to give him the bones of humans from the previous world. The worms helped Quetzalcoatl by perforating the shell. They also created a concoction to cure impotency that included white firm worms as one of the principal ingredients.[130]

Nonordinary Realm Associations: Middleworld and Underworld
Spiritual and Shapeshifting Medicine: catharsis, pragmatism, intuition, and resilience

Symbolism Meanings

◄ You have everything you need to make your goals happen; trust yourself.

◄ Be creative in shifting any circumstances that seem less than ideal. The universe will surprise you with something beyond anything that you could have imagined.

◄ Volunteer to help others that could use a helping hand, and allow your heart to continue to open up to more compassion.

◄ Use your empathic gifts to guide you to more positive people and circumstances.

❀ Falcon ❀

The falcon was a common symbol of the reborn sun at dawn, and it was admired for being an excellent hunter.[131] In the Popol Vuh, the falcon played a role as a chain messenger when the Hero Twins were summoned into the Underworld. The falcon had swallowed a snake that had swallowed a toad that had swallowed a louse that had swallowed a message from the twins' grandmother.[132] The louse represented corruption and decay. The toad was associated with the watery Underworld and the fertility of the earth's interior as a source of renewal. The serpent was a common symbol of regeneration because of its tendency to periodically shed its old skin to uncover a new one. Finally, the falcon was the rebirth of the sun at dawn. The sequence of animals likely foretells the death and corruption of the Hero Twins in the Underworld, followed by their rebirth to new life and apotheosis as the sun and moon.[133]

Perhaps due to its exceptional vision, the falcon, specifically the laughing falcon, had curative gifts and was an omen for dry and rainy seasons.[134] The call of the laughing falcon (ha-ha-ha), which mimics the Yucatec Mayan word *ha'*, meaning "water," is thought to be an omen for rain.[135] Sahagún states the Mexica believed that the call "*huac, huac!*" or "*yeccan, yeccan!*" were taken respectively to mean, "dry, dry!" or "good weather, good weather!"[136] The Central Mexicans also used the bones of the laughing falcon as a remedy for pain caused in any part of the body by torn flesh. The fumes of its burned feathers were also used to restore sanity to persons deranged by severe illness.[137]

Nonordinary Realm Associations: Upperworld and Middleworld
Spiritual and Shapeshifting Medicine: clairvoyance, healing, prophecy, and shrewdness
Symbolism Meanings

◄ You are a natural healer. Continue to develop your healing gifts, and remember, you can apply them in many ways.

◄ When manifesting your dreams, do not allow fear and its ugly cousins, doubt and insecurities, get in the way. Be the fierce hunter in pursuing and manifesting them.

◄ There is a situation that you need to step away from and assess as a detached, objective, and present observer. Once you have done so, reassess it, and then bring your insight to the table.

◄ Trust your intuition; it will always guide you in the right direction.

❋ Feathered or Plumed Serpent ❋

The mythological feathered serpent was a rather pervasive image throughout Mesoamerica, and its meanings and understandings were polysemic and complex. The feathered serpent could be a deity known as Quetzalcoatl (Central Mexico), Kukulkan (Yucatec Mayan), or Gucumatz (K'iché' Maya)) or a mythological zoomorphic animal. Rulers, such as the Toltec ruler Topiltzin-Quetzalcoatl, also took on the name and essence of this mythological animal and deity. The feathered serpent, most likely the deity, was associated with transforming into the morning star and was thought to be able to take the actual form of a feathered serpent.[138]

The feathered serpent also served as a conduit to the floral paradise, where ancestors and brave warriors would oftentimes be deified. During the Postclassic period, the Central Mexicans also believed that with the help of brave warriors and royal ancestors, the feathered serpent would sweep the way for the sun at dawn and ensure it reached its daily zenith.[139] The feathered serpent was often depicted releasing animating soul energies from its mouth or nose and was a symbol of transformation: both birds and serpents come into the world as eggs but then transform into very different animals.[140]

Nonordinary Realm Associations: Upperworld and Middleworld

Spiritual and Shapeshifting Medicine: wisdom, creativity, inspiration, and metamorphosis

Symbolism Meanings

◄ Pathways are being opened up for great positive transformation. Make sure you are ready, and clear any possible limiting beliefs of being unworthy.

◄ Provide yourself with the time and space to learn something new that you have been interested in. Continue to diversify your skills and talents, and find ways to put them to use. New, ideal opportunities will come of this.

◄ Exercise your imagination and creativity through writing, visualization exercises, drawing, or some other art or craft-oriented activity. Imagination and creativity are muscles that need to and should be exercised to continue to open up to divine inspiration.

◄ Learn to flow with change and transformation; your overall success and spiritual growth will continue to flourish as a result.

☀ Firefly ☀

Fireflies were associated with the ritual practice of smoking cigars and were often depicted in Classic Maya vases smoking cigars. At Classic period sites Tikal and Dos Pilas, there are references to a deity that seems to have been particularly important to the dynasty of these cities, and one that may have originated in the early history of Tikal.[141] This deity has a firefly head, is smoking a cigar, and is associated with the Underworld.[142]

In the Book of Chilam Balam of Chumayel, *firefly* was a ritual term for a cigar or smoking tube. Fireflies were also metaphors for stars.[143]

In the Popol Vuh, when the lords of the Underworld were testing the Hero Twins in the Dark House, one of the layers of the Underworld, fireflies helped the twins defeat the lords and pass the test. The lords gave the Hero Twins cigars and demanded that they smoke them. However, the lords also ordered them to return the next morning with the cigars unburned, or they would be sacrificed as punishment. The Hero Twins placed fireflies at the tips of the cigars to imitate burning and pretended to smoke them all night. The Hero Twins passed this test.[144]

Nonordinary Realm Associations: Underworld
Spiritual and Shapeshifting Medicine: illumination, confidence, magic, and enchantment
Symbolism Meanings

◂ Find inspiration, wonderment, and awe in the smallest of things. This minor investment will result in abundant beauty and grace on many levels.

◂ You have been putting in the practical work and effort, but do not forget to work your magic as well.

◂ Be a shining example of light, hope, and inspiration for your family, friends, and loved ones. This will continue to expand your own light and intuitive gifts.

◂ Be confident in your gifts, talents, and skills. You bring more to the table than you think.

❂ Fox ❂

Foxes were seen as cunning, troublesome nocturnal animals. Like coyotes, they were known for discovering and digging up hidden or secret things and were principally solitary rather than pack animals.[145] In the Book of Chilam Balam of Chumayel, they were associated with draining people financially.[146] In the Popol Vuh, foxes along with various other

animals were responsible for being tricksters. After the Hero Twins had spent a day clearing a field for the planting of maize, the foxes joined deer, rabbit, coyote, peccary, coati, and many birds to raise the field in a single night and make it look as if the twins had not cleared the field.[147]

Nonordinary Realm Associations: Underworld
Spiritual and Shapeshifting Medicine: cleverness, wildness, tracking, and clairaudience
Symbolism Meanings

◄ It is wise to keep your plans to yourself, even if you are excited about them. Not everyone will be genuinely happy for you.

◄ Give yourself some time to be alone and reflect on your next steps.

◄ Take the time to intuitively listen to the needs and feelings of loved ones, friends, and family; you will learn a lot more than you could have imagined.

◄ Be discerning; someone is not being forthcoming and is hiding pertinent information from you.

☀ Frog ☀

The ability of frogs to lay thousands of eggs and typically in water strongly connected them with fertility, the beginning of a cycle, water, and entrances to the Underworld. Croaking frogs were usually a sign of coming rain, often appeared in rain imagery, and were linked to Chaac, the Maya rain deity, and Tlaloc, the Central Mexican rain deity.

The Maya saw them as the musicians of Chaac.[148] In Classic period site Copan there is a small complex south of the Copan River with frog sculptures, denoting an entrance to the Underworld through the river.[149]

Frogs were also associated with the moon since the moon controls bodies of water. One of the titles of the moon in Yucatec Mayan is Virgin Rain Frog.[150] The upended frog glyph (T740) often made reference to the beginning of a lifetime or marked the first lunar crescent moon.[151] At Classic period site Balamku, stucco sculpture segments A–C of the superstructure building include a full figure "birth frog," upon which sits a ruler in the guise of the maize deity, denoting a metaphorical birth of a deity.[152]

Frogs, however, could have less than favorable connotations. When Central Mexican peoples found frogs or toads on the roof of their houses, they considered this a warning sign and consulted their local curanderx.[153]

In many contemporary Yucatec villages, the people engage in a "bring rain" ceremony, where they have young boys croak like frogs to entice the coming of rain.[154] During the ceremony four young boys are tied to the posts at the four wooden altar corners, associated with the four cardinal directions and colors. They place large offerings of fruit, corn, and bread on the altar. The young boys then typically crouch under the altar and throughout the ceremony croak like frogs.[155]

Nonordinary Realm Associations: Middleworld and Underworld
Spiritual and Shapeshifting Medicine: incitement, vigor, abundance, and prognostication
Symbolism Meanings

◄ The time is ripe for rebirth and renewal; delve into it and make the most of it.

◄ Your hard work is about to pay off; you are about to enter a season of abundance.

◄ You have the skills and ability to be an inspirational leader and incite positive action; use them.

◄ Work on your throat chakra through toning or singing; there are some unsaid things that need to come out with patience and sweetness.

☀ Gopher ☀

Gophers' powerful claws allow them to dig deep burrows underground and forage for roots and insects. Due to their subterranean nature, they were believed to be able to carry messages to the Underworld and were largely associated with the buried dead. Their ability to store food in their cheeks could be why they were also often associated with the earth's bounty.[156]

In many depictions of an anthropomorphic gopher, the being is holding an ak'bal vessel.[157] These vessels were often held by human shapeshifters, animal coessences, and animal guides. Ak'bal as noted means night and power. The vessel was likely holding the animating soul energy of the transformative energies the night sun was believed to emit. It may have catalyzed the transformation into an animal or strengthened the connection to an animal spirit guide.[158]

Nonordinary Realm Associations: Middleworld and Underworld
Spiritual and Shapeshifting Medicine: persistence, investigation, tenacity, and prudence
Symbolism Meanings

◄ It is time for some spring cleaning. Let go of items that you have been hoarding and have not been using, possibly by gifting them to a charity or friends.

◄ Be prudent. There are unseen forces—jealousy and gossip—attempting to uproot the work you have done. Remove these forces from your environment and make no exceptions.

◄ Be diligent and persistent in getting to the truth of a matter and listen to your intuition in the process.

◄ Build your savings account and vision of where you can continue to save and put away money.

❀ Hawk ❀

Hawks were highly admired for their superb hunting skills and sharp vision, which is probably why rulers and curanderx often appropriated hawk features in their dress and accoutrements.[159] In the Central Mexican Codex Borgia, hawks, along with other raptors such as owls and eagles, were depicted in the illustrations associated with the dry seasons of the year. The onset of the dry season takes place on page 45 of the codex, where we see the hunting deity, Camaxtli, standing on a skull rack, holding a shield, a dart thrower, a war banner, and a net for carrying game. Behind him, a tree with dark mirrors is topped by war banners, symbolizing the season of warfare beginning in November with the onset of the dry season. On the rooftops of three of the four temples there is a hawk, an eagle, and an owl, and the fourth likely has down feathers,* probably also another raptor. The temples topped by raptors also represent the dry season, the season of warfare.[160]

In the Legend of the Suns, the hawk was one of the animals that went after Nanahuatzin when he threw himself into the fiery hearth. Although courageous, the hawk was unable to lift him out and was discolored by smoke.[161] Because they are diurnal animals, hawks are also typically associated with the sun.

Nonordinary Realm Associations: Upperworld
Spiritual and Shapeshifting Medicine: clairvoyance, perception, predatory nature, and boldness
Symbolism Meanings

- ◄ Be honest with yourself about your level of happiness and contentment and be more open to new opportunities and trying new things.
- ◄ Stand back and observe any conflicting or unclear situations from a more detached and objective prospective.

---

*Down feathers are feathers found under tougher exterior feathers and are often used in limpia ceremonies.

◄ New ideal opportunities are on the horizon that will provide growth in many ways.

◄ You have been patient and on the lookout. It is time to act on what you have found. Go for it!

❀ Heron ❀

Due to the heron's superb abilities to fly, spear into water, and quickly catch fish, it was highly revered and associated with creator deities, and rulers that associated themselves with these deities. The well-preserved hieroglyphs at Temple XIX at Palenque, for example, denote a possible rebirth of GI, a principal creator deity, on the same day of the seating of ruler K'inich Ahkal Mo' Nahb. On the day of the ruler's accession, he is depicted as wearing distinctive emblems associated with deity GI, including a small heron grasping a fish in its beak. The Maya chose the date of the ruler's accession to evoke cosmological significance. His accession took place on 9 ik, which was also the mythological date of the enthronement of GI. The ruler relied on GI's creation story to legitimize his reign religiously and politically.[162] The heron emblem glyph identified the lords of Palenque as the "sacred lords of the lineage of the white heron."[163]

On Kerr Vase 4331, the heron in the first image may be creating or giving birth to the Cacao, the maize deity, through its mouth. Emerging from the mouth of an animal is a common visual metaphor for transformation, accession, and conjuring,[164] as are the heron's access into the watery Underworld, its habit of bringing its game to the Middleworld, and its ability to fly into the Upperworld.

In Central Mexico, Tezcatlipoca's idol and his penitents often wore heron feathers.[165] Their principal rain and lightning deity, Tlaloc, was often depicted with herons and water-dwelling creatures.[166] One of the four cities of the Tlaxcalteca bore the name Ticatlan, and its chief was Aztaua, "owner of the heron."[167]

Nonordinary Realm Associations: Upperworld, Middleworld, and Underworld

Spiritual and Shapeshifting Medicine: rebirth, catharsis, dexterity, and resourcefulness

Symbolism Meanings

- ◄ Trust in your abilities and skills to seamlessly move past anything that may seem like an obstacle.
- ◄ Take time to engage in rites to connect with your ancestors. They have insight, guidance, and medicine that will help you.
- ◄ Listen to your intuition as to when to move forward. When you get a sense that it is time, do so without questioning your resolve.
- ◄ Question and think critically, but remain humble, and be open to input from others.

❁ Hummingbird ❁

Hummingbirds were associated with the sun, love, war, resurrection, and fertility—due to their role as pollinators of plants.[168] They are small diurnal birds with beautiful iridescent feathers, and they are the only birds that can fly backward. They are known for performing aerial acrobatics and quickly darting back and forth, making them look like glints of sunlight.[169] Although they are rather small, they are also known to be territorial and aggressive fighters.[170] When they sleep they enter torpor, and they can stay in this state for prolonged periods—a day or more and sometimes an entire season. Torpor is a deep sleep, wherein their body temperature drops to the point of becoming hypothermic, their heart rate and their breathing slow down significantly, and they save up to 60 percent of their available energy. When they are in torpor it looks as if they are dead.

Sahagún and Duran both wrote about the hummingbird's torpor capabilities and related associations with death and rebirth. They said that in winter hummingbirds would stick their bills in a tree. When the tree rejuvenated, the hummingbird would grow feathers, awaken, and be reborn.[171] Both the Maya and Central Mexican peoples often depicted hummingbirds in a floral paradise. Sahagún also wrote that the Central Mexican peoples believed that four years after their death, brave warriors would become hummingbirds, birds, or butterflies, and spend the rest of eternity drinking nectar from flowers in Upperworld and on earth.[172]

The Mexica's tutelary war deity, Huitzilopochtli, was commonly depicted with a blue-green hummingbird headdress, likely due to the birds' aforementioned associations with the death and the resurrection of brave warriors as hummingbirds.[173] In the Codex Borgia, hummingbirds were illustrated in scenes associated with the rainy season and an abundance of maize and flowers.[174]

In Classic Maya art, the sun often courted the moon in the form of a hummingbird and possibly a mosquito, which was likely regarded as the counterpart to a hummingbird.[175] In modern narratives, the sun suitor takes the shape of a hummingbird. On Classic Maya Vase 504, creator deity Itzamna and the young moon goddess sit on a celestial throne marked by a sky band along the edge. A young man occupies a lower unmarked bench and holds up a vase, perhaps presenting it to Itzamna. The curved beak that projects from the front of his face, pricking through a flower, is probably a hummingbird mask, which suggests that he is the hummingbird suitor, presenting respects to his potential father-in-law.[176] On the Postclassic Dresden Codex 7b, the hummingbird is identified as the *chich,* "prophecy," of several gods, indicating its role as a messenger of the gods.[177]

Nonordinary Realm Associations: Upperworld and Middleworld
Spiritual and Shapeshifting Medicine: bravery, joy, acrobatics, and
   rebirth

Symbolism Meanings

- ◄ You have mighty divine forces helping you. Have faith, and keep it light.

- ◄ Do not forget the importance and power of joyfulness and playfulness. Give yourself opportunities to practice these invaluable skills.

- ◄ Be relentless in pursuing your goals, and go beyond believing you can do something; know that you can.

- ◄ Remember to give yourself time to conserve your energy and rest; be strategic and intentional about this. When you are resting, do not answer business-related calls, emails, or texts; simply rest.

◉ Iguana-Lizard ◉

There are over six thousand species of lizards. The lizard (*cuetzpallin*) was the fourth day sign of the Mexica's tonalpohualli and was associated with the south. Those born under this day sign were said to be fortunate, were destined to be wealthy, and would never be hungry, as they were perceived as being calm and patient, while their food came to them.[178] Due to a lizard's ability to lose its tail and grow another one, it was thought to be able to wisely detach, when necessary. Lizards were also thought of as being particularly resilient, since they were able to survive falls and go two to five days without eating.[179]

Iguanas, a species of lizard, were particularly important to the Maya. They are one of the animal avatars of Maya creator deity Itzamna.[180] It was believed that the world sat within a house of four walls, and each wall was a tremendous iguana and was associated with a particular color and cardinal direction. The tips of the iguana came together to form the sky or the ceiling of the house, and the house was called Itzamna, meaning Iguana House.[181] Three incised bones found at Classic period site Tikal show four animal figures with anthropomorphic attributes: an iguana, a spider monkey, a parrot, and a dog, all of which remain in the same order in all three scenes, with a pair of Paddler Gods steering the canoe. These animals were principal characters of what the bones were likely depicting, cosmic creation scenes.[182]

Nonordinary Realm Associations: Upperworld and Middleworld

Spiritual and Shapeshifting Medicine: perception, camouflage, serenity, and patience

Symbolism Meanings

◄ Let yourself be still, observe, and then assess your surroundings before making your next move.

◄ Connect with spirit of lizards, trees, or eclipses, and thank them for teaching you how to camouflage and manage your energy. This way you can avoid unwanted scenarios and attract more beneficial ones.

◄ Remember to enjoy the simple things in life, especially nature, and let them remind you of what you are grateful for.

◄ Break free from old stories and identities that are binding you, and create more favorable ones.

☀ Jaguar ☀

The Jaguar was the animal that rulers, curanderx, and sorcerers most commonly associated themselves with, likely due to its special night vision and formidable prowess. Jaguars are the largest and most powerful feline in the Americas.[183] They are incredibly skilled hunters, swimmers, and tree climbers and often stalk their prey along waterways or hunt from trees. They typically sleep in caves and crevices, places that are associated with portals, the Underworld, and spaces of creation.[184]

There are a number of Classic Maya jaguar deities that are identified with the night sun. During the night, the sun deity journeyed through the Underworld in his manifestation as the fearsome jaguar god.[185] The jaguar god of the Underworld is typically shown with spotted feline ears, a central pointed fang, spiral eyes, and a thin line that runs beneath the squared eyes and twists to form a curl, identified as the "cruller" on the bridge of the nose or the brow.[186] Deity GIII from

Palenque may be a conflation of the jaguar god of the Underworld. His shrine is the Temple of the Sun, indicating that GIII was the warrior sun, tied closely to the Underworld.[187] The scene panel of the Temple of the Sun depicts a cave within the earth—the Underworld into which GIII journeys every night.[188]

Maya deities were often depicted sitting on jaguar thrones and wore jaguar pelts or had jaguar features, such as jaguar ears or feline canines. Deity O, an elderly lunar-related deity, for example, frequently appears with jaguar claws, fangs, and a jaguar eye.[189] Rulers were also shown sitting on jaguar thrones and wearing jaguar-skin garments in combat.[190] In the Classic period inscriptions, the hieroglyph way (animal coessence) consisted of a stylized human face, or possibly an ajaw face, partially covered by jaguar skin. The jaguar as a way, or animal guide, has been illustrated with many different aspects, including water, fire, clouds, waterlilies, the moon, a paddler, and war.[191]

The Mexica saw the jaguar as one of the strongest and bravest animals, the companion of the eagle. Eagle and jaguar or *quauhtli-ocelotl* (in Nahuatl) was the conventionalized designation for the highest-ranking warriors.[192] In the Legend of the Suns, after Nanahuatzin threw himself into the fiery hearth, the jaguar was one of the courageous animals that went into the hearth to try to carry him out. But he was unable to do so and became spotted from the fire in the process.[193]

The Mexica also identified the jaguar with the night and the Underworld and associated it with darkness.[194] It was one of the animals that was associated with eating the sun at solar eclipses. In his guise as a jaguar, Tezcatlipoca, the patron deity of the nahualtin (shapeshifters), was identified as Tepeyollotl, "heart of the mountains."[195] Jaguar (ocelotl) is the fourteenth day sign in the Mexica's tonalpohualli and was associated with the north. Those born under jaguar were said to be courageous, daring, haughty, presumptuous, proud, conceited, and grave.[196]

Nonordinary Realm Associations: Underworld

Spiritual and Shapeshifting Medicine: power, clairvoyance, courage, and stealth

Symbolism Meanings

- ◄ Develop a strong sense of self, and acknowledge and embody your talents, skills, and experience.
- ◄ Be stealthy, strategic, and courageous in pursuing your goals. You are on the right path.
- ◄ You are naturally clairvoyant. Practice developing your clairvoyant skills by strengthening your visual imagination muscles during meditations and trance journeys.
- ◄ Stay quiet, and observe circumstances from afar. Trust your intuition as to what you are sensing. Once you have assessed matters, make a swift decision.

❂ Lovely Cotinga ❂

The lovely cotinga is a dovelike tropical bird with turquoise-blue plumage and a purple breast and throat. Its brilliant colored feathers were believed to emanate animating soul energy when they were used and worn.[197] According to the Annals of the Cakchiquels, the highly prized feathers of the lovely cotinga were given as tribute to the lords of Tulan in the east.[198] In the Popol Vuh, the creators, the Framer and the Shaper, Sovereign and Quetzal Serpent were in water cradled in precious quetzal and lovely cotinga feathers and, by extension, wrapped in animating soul energy.[199] A prayer recorded by Sahagún also describes Mexica conceptions of Huehueteotl-Xiuhtecuhtli, the mother and father of the gods, also being in water wrapped in lovely cotinga feathers within the navel of the earth.[200]

Nonordinary Realm Associations: Upperworld
Spiritual and Shapeshifting Medicine: invigoration, allure, elegance, and admiration
Symbolism Meanings

◄ Have faith; you are being divinely supported and cared for.

◄ Pursue your goals knowing that you are worthy of all the happiness, joy, and success this life has to offer, and let go of any feelings or beliefs of not being worthy.

◄ Gift yourself some time to be pampered and praised; you deserve it.

◄ Reflect on your emotions and actions, and make sure they are aligned with your goals.

✿ Macaw ✿

Macaws are very social birds and were commonly domesticated. They were revered for their beautiful brilliant-colored feathers and long tail feathers.[201] Likely due to their diurnal nature and their habit of waking up with the sun to search for food, they were often associated with Mesoamerican solar deities.[202] In Postclassic Izamal, Yucatán, K'inich K'ak Mo' Nahb, the sun deity of Izamal, was known to shapeshift into a macaw at noon with the fiery rays of the sun to consume the offerings made by people suffering from illness.[203] In other instances, it was said that the sun deity would burn the offerings with bolts of fire.[204] It was believed that these consumed or burned offerings would inspire this solar deity to help heal the petitioners. Postclassic codices illustrate a macaw carrying a fiery torch, which may have signaled periods of drought or too much sun.[205]

Nonordinary Realm Associations: Upperworld
Spiritual and Shapeshifting Medicine: healing, boldness, distinction, and sociability

Symbolism Meanings

◄ Let yourself shine, and flaunt your unique skills and talents; stop hiding or suppressing them.

◄ Get outside your comfort zone of friends, and expand your circles. You will not only learn more about yourself, but you will likely embark on new opportunities.

◄ Consider doing important tasks in the earlier mornings; you may be more productive at this time.

◄ People are becoming more receptive to what you have to say. Continue to develop your charismatic and inspirational speaking skills; they are going to serve you greatly in your next venture.

❁ Monkey ❁

Monkeys were strongly associated with the arts—singing, dancing, and sculpture. In myths, monkeys were often identified as the failed attempt to create humans or were human beings turned into monkeys because of their disobedience. Monkeys were also often domesticated.[206]

The Maya attributed solar symbolism to monkeys likely because the monkeys native to these regions were diurnal and had a tendency to jump, leap, and reside in trees. In Classic Maya artwork, monkey gods are often depicted as artists, scribes, and sages reading or writing in open books, painting, dancing, and making music. These monkey gods were associated with the priestly and ruling class who claimed the privilege of learning hieroglyphics.[207] Scribes and artists ranked high in Maya society and were a privileged class. In their artwork, it was typically the black-handed spider monkey and the large howler monkey who were artists and patrons of the arts. Howler monkeys have an exceptional range of vocalizations, which likely contributes to their musical associations. The spider monkey is incredibly acrobatic and graceful.[208] Due to their some-what mischievous nature, monkeys were also paired with cacao due to its reputation for being a stimulant and an intoxicant during festivities.[209]

In the Popol Vuh, the Hero Twins were mistreated by their elder brothers, who gave them almost no food and even tried to kill them. The Hero Twins tricked their elder brothers into climbing a tree to get a bird down and then had them turned into monkeys. As monkeys, they danced and performed acrobatics while the Hero Twins played a song.[210] Their names refer to two different types of monkeys: Hun Batz, a howler monkey, and Hun Chuen, a spider monkey. After being defeated by the Hero Twins, they become deified and were described as men of genius and as flautists, singers, writers, and carvers.[211]

In the Legend of the Suns, the second world known as 4-Wind was destroyed by Tezcatlipoca. Quetzalcoatl, the wind god, and his race of people were carried off by fierce winds. The descendants of this race became monkeys. Codex Vaticanus A illustrates this world being ended by violent winds, with Quetzalcoatl represented as regent and monkeys leaping among clouds of dust.[212]

The monkey (*ozomahtli*) is the eleventh day of the tonalpohualli and was associated with the west. Those born on the day of monkey were fated to be actors and singers and graceful and clever.[213] Along with their skills in the arts in general, monkeys were also linked with forbidden pleasure and sin.[214]

Nonordinary Realm Associations: Upperworld and Middleworld
Spiritual and Shapeshifting Medicine: artistic ability, culture, play, and outgoingness
Symbolism Meanings

- Make more time for personal creative artistic endeavors to help you become more clear and focused and excited about your path and life in general.
- There are changes coming. Although they may seem undesirable, trust in your skills in grasping and jumping to places you need to be with great skill and grace. It is time to get out of your comfort zone.
- Think outside the box, and create spaces to flaunt and showcase your creative skills and abilities.

◄ Release blocks to expressing yourself in healthy assertive ways through breathwork coupled with toning, singing, or primal vocal releases.

❀ Mouse ❀

Mice are generally smaller than rats with pointed snouts, small rounded ears, and body-length scaly tails. Like rats, they have a high breeding rate and are nocturnal rodents that live in in-between spaces. A female mouse gets pregnant five to ten times a year and can give birth to a litter of three to fourteen mice. Although they have poor eyesight, they have excellent hearing and a keen sense of smell, which they rely on to locate food and avoid predators. They were known to cause grave damage and destroy precious things because they easily hid in homes and reproduced fairly quickly. They were also known as eavesdroppers that acquired information and inquired into one's affairs.[215] Often when they were seen in a home it was thought that adultery was taking place.[216]

Nonordinary Realm Associations: Middleworld and Underworld
Spiritual and Shapeshifting Medicine: resourcefulness, fertility, eavesdropping, and prudence
Symbolism Meanings
 ◄ It is time to stop and reassess your circumstances. You have been turning a blind eye to something that needs your attention.
 ◄ You are underestimating your talents and skills.
 ◄ Trust your intuition on when to take action.
 ◄ It is time to come out of the shadows and go after what you desire.

❀ New World Quail ❀

New World quail are small birds with dark plumage strewn with small white spots and short but typically strong legs. They had lunar, earth, and fertility associations, and the lunar and earth-related Central Mexican deities, Tlazolteotl and Xipe Totec, were often depicted with quail feathers or would have an entire quail as an ornament.[217] Central Mexican codices typically depicted stars as eyespots, so these birds were symbols of the starry sky, as the white spots on their plumage were believed to resemble the eyespots associated with the stars. The Central Mexican peoples called these birds *yollototl* (heart bird) and believed that when we died our hearts turned into them. It was also believed that their singing gladdened and consoled the heart.[218]

New World quail are very intelligent, largely terrestrial birds that are reluctant to fly and prefer to walk, run, or hide from danger. They tend to live in flocks and feed from what they find on the ground: insects, seeds, vegetation, and tubers. Even the tree quails that nest in high trees generally feed on the ground. Their higher clutch sizes, ranging from three to six eggs for the tree quail and wood quail and ten to fifteen for the northern bobwhite, likely gave them fertility, vegetation, and Middleworld associations.

Perhaps their tendency and preference to stay on the ground and eat insects coming from the inside of the earth also gave them connections with Mictlantecuhtli. In the Legend of the Suns, after Mictlantecuhtli gave Quetzalcoatl the bones he sought and then regretted his decision, it was a quail that aided him in intercepting Quetzalcoatl. The intelligent quail frightened Quetzalcoatl, and as a result the bones fell down and were broken into pieces.[219]

Nonordinary Realm Associations: Upperworld, Middleworld, and Underworld

Spiritual and Shapeshifting Medicine: covertness, resourcefulness, family connections, and productivity

Symbolism Meanings

◄ Everything you need for your next task is within reach through the connections you have already made or resources you have at your disposal. Do not create unnecessary work for yourself.

- Make time to be nurtured, supported, and uplifted by soul or blood family.
- You have a gift for inspiring others through the wisdom of your words. Share this invaluable gift.
- Abundant new beginnings are waiting for you. Gather your resources and take advantage of this period.

ꙮ Ocelot (Cat) ꙮ

Ocelots are medium-sized wild cats weighing eighteen to thirty-four pounds. They are typically active during twilight and nighttime and are known to be solitary and territorial. The Central Mexican peoples thought of them as cautious, wise, noble, reserved, and well kept and might have domesticated them. Like domesticated cats, they bathe, clean, and wash themselves with their tongues. They see very well in the dark, which makes them excellent hunters of other small terrestrial mammals, such as armadillos and opossums. Because ocelots were thought to have fortuitous magical powers, sorcerers were known to carry the hide of their forehead, chest, tail, nose, claws, fangs, and snout. Along with magical powers, these items were believed to give people courage.[220]

Nonordinary Realm Associations: Underworld

Spiritual and Shapeshifting Medicine: regalness, predatory instincts, independence, and magic

Symbolism Meanings
- Strengthen your connection to animal magic. One way of doing so is by creating a medicine bundle. Gather a beautiful fabric or hide, and place into it pictures of the animals you choose to connect with or items relating to them that were acquired ethically. Place other offerings that you feel the animals would like inside as well.
- Let yourself do some independent soul searching as to what your best course of action is. Trust your inner guidance and intuition.

◄ You are naturally gifted with magical influence and know how to work magic intuitively. Ask for the ideal in your magical rites, and let the universe surprise and wow you.

◄ It is time to step up and be courageous. Once you have taken the time to intuitively observe and assess circumstances, step up and firmly stand your ground.

◈ Opossum ◈

Opossums have two to three litters of young a year, which is perhaps why they were identified with creators and were metaphors for the dying and reviving year.[221] They were also known for being thieves, who terrorized chicken coops.[222] Their fertility and trickster associations played out in recurring roles in stories and myths, such as chiefs of the world, the shattered one who reconstitutes himself, the shrewd character who faces jaguars, the leader of the wise old counselors, and a respected wise grandfather.[223] They also had Underworld links because they are nocturnal animals.[224]

The opossum is mentioned as a ritual clown in the colonial Book of Chilam Balam of Tizimin.[225] In the Popol Vuh, the opossum is depicted as a lord of the half-light of the preceding dawn, or as a representation of the gods who hold up the sky at each of the four corners of the world.[226] In addition, the opossum was known for swindling fire from divine forces for the benefit of humans.

In the Central Mexican codices Fejervary Mayer, Vindobonensis, Vaticanus B, Dresden, and Nuttall, opossums were linked with the ball game, crossroads leading into the Underworld, decapitation, New Year ceremonies, the moon, and pulque.[227] They were also the model for mothers, since opossum mothers carried their numerous young in their pouch and were known to shed tears if they were taken from their young. Additionally, they served as important medicine. Opossum tail was known to clear blockages of the urine and other body liquids and phlegm due to coughs and constipation and was used for women having difficulty in childbirth.[228]

Nonordinary Realm Associations: Middleworld and Underworld

Spiritual and Shapeshifting Medicine: fertility, regeneration, nurturing, and shrewdness

Symbolism Meanings

- ◄ Refrain from showing all your cards, including ones relating to your good fortune.
- ◄ Take action to clear self-limiting beliefs one step at a time. It is time to get out of your comfort zone and step up to your true potential.
- ◄ Let yourself be nurtured and cared for; you deserve it.
- ◄ You may have to boast about your skills and experience, and it may feel like bragging. But it will open an opportunity to do something you know in your heart you can do.

❂ Owl ❂

The nocturnal owl, with its excellent night vision and formidable skill as a swift-flying predator in the dark, was strongly linked to the Underworld, night, darkness, warriors, and death and was often the messenger of Underworld deities.[229] Similar to hawks, eagles, and falcons, they kill their prey with their talons.[230]

In some codices, the principal Yucatec Maya death deity, Yum Cimil, is painted as half owl and half human.[231] In the Popol Vuh, when Underworld maiden Xquic is cast out from the Underworld due to her pregnancy, she convinces the owl, messenger of the Underworld, to spare her. The owl leads her to the surface of the earth, where she eventually gives birth to the Hero Twins.[232] Screech owls in particular were emissaries of the lords of the Underworld.[233] Deity L, an Underworld Maya merchant deity, typically fashioned a large hat trimmed with a screech owl that had black-tipped feathers. The screech owl was also closely identified with rain and the Maya rain deity Chaac.[234]

In Nahuatl, the most common name for a sorcerer was *tlacatecolotl* (owl man).[235] If an owl called out above a home or from a nearby tree, two or three times, it was believed that someone was going to become ill or die, especially if someone in the home was already ill. A call from a horned owl was an omen that precipitated total destruction of one's house.[236] If someone had a dream of a barn owl entering their home, it was believed the person would commit adultery.[237]

Nonordinary Realm Associations: Underworld

Spiritual and Shapeshifting Medicine: virtue, wisdom, courage, and magic

Symbolism Meanings

- ◄ Your intuitive prophetic gifts are being awakened; notice how they are making themselves known to you.

- ◄ Pay attention to the messages that are coming forth from your unconscious and subconscious via dreams, meditations, trance journeys, and daydreams; there is something unresolved that needs your attention.

- ◄ You are an excellent judge of character; trust your intuition, especially if you feel someone is keeping something from you or is not telling you the full truth.

- ◄ While you may be going through what feels like a difficult phase in your life, be courageous. Listen to your intuition as to what feels out of alignment or stagnant and begin to shift out of it. Once you do, you will find that graceful pathways will open up for you, and you will begin to integrate the lessons with greater ease.

✺ Peccary ✺

Peccaries have flexible snouts, pointed hoofs, and relatively tough skin and are known for being able to defend themselves, especially when travelling in packs. Perhaps because they were used as a food delicacy and in ritual, they were associated with fertility, abundance, and renewal. They were often portrayed with the Maya sun and maize deities.[238] Peccaries were depicted as a mode of transportation for the sun during the rainy long summer days.[239] Itzamna was also often seen riding a peccary.[240]

In Classic Maya art, "fire peccaries" were prominent actors and may have been graphic representations of powerful ecstatic howls of individuals transforming into an animal through ritual intoxication. Loud vocalizations were common during ritual use of entheogens.[241] There are a number of vessels that depict a peccary with flame-like projections emerging from its nostrils and wearing a death's eye collar or scarf around its neck.[242] Classic Maya Vase 1203 depicts a monkey and peccary toppled in a position suggesting intoxication via an enema tube. Enema funnels were used to increase the volume of intoxicants administered and hastened inebriation.[243]

Nonordinary Realm Associations: Middleworld and Underworld
Spiritual and Shapeshifting Medicine: toughness, loyalty, bravery, and renewal

Symbolism Meanings

◄ Develop a thick skin and speak your truth with love and compassion. Refrain from internalizing anything that offends you.

◄ Own your strength with confidence, grace, and humility.

◄ Let yourself ask for help from others when you need it. You do not have to do everything on your own.

◄ Be grateful for those who are loyal to you, and let them know how much you appreciate them.

✹ Pelican ✹

Pelicans travel in flocks and hunt tenaciously and cooperatively. They are able to hold about three gallons of water in their pouch-like beak and immediately swallow fish upon catching them. Perhaps due to their larger stature, fearless hunting style, and, on average, ten-foot wing span, Central Mexicans identified them as the leaders of all the waterbirds. They were said to be the heart of the water and summoned the wind by crying out. A flock of white pelicans can create a whirlpool when dozens of them, maybe even hundreds, fly helically. This is likely why they were associated with the wind and Central Mexican wind deity, Ehecatl-Quetzalcoatl.[244] People that lived by the water believed that pelicans had a divinatory green stone in their gizzard and various precious feathers. If a hunter was not able to find the green stone or the precious feathers, bad luck would befall the hunter.[245]

Nonordinary Realm Associations: Upperworld, Middleworld, and Underworld

Spiritual and Shapeshifting Medicine: collaboration, boldness, persistence, and nobility

Symbolism Meanings

◄ When taking on more than you think you can handle, fine-tune your ability to prioritize, let go of inconsequential matters, and when necessary, learn to say no without hesitation. Handle your business like a boss.

◄ You are multitalented. Believe in yourself, and give yourself the opportunity to delve into diverse environments and ventures.

◄ Collaborate with like-hearted and like-minded people, and bring your skills and talents together, as a community; all of you will thrive.

◄ Be fearless, bold, and tenacious in realizing your dreams.

❀ Porcupine ❀

In codices, porcupines were often illustrated as symbols of light bodies that emitted rays, likely due to the belief that they could shoot quills from their bodies. They have roughly thirty thousand quills covering most of their body and tucked inside their long strands of brown hair. The quills can get lodged in a predator's skin and swell up with body heat, making them more painful to take out. Although the quills are not shot out, they may fly out when a porcupine shakes its body, and they can be released on contact. Porcupines were associated with water and the moon, possibly because when they are not living in the trees of the forests, they live in the undergrowth alongside lakes and rivers. Their quills are hollow, which allows them to float on water. The Central Mexicans saw porcupines as a kind of playful yet sometimes mischievous sprite.[246]

Nonordinary Realm Associations: Middleworld and Underworld
Spiritual and Shapeshifting Medicine: curiosity, playfulness, innocence, and resourcefulness
Symbolism Meanings

◄ Stop taking yourself so seriously. Let yourself be silly and playful, and have fun!

◄ If negative energies and people continue to invade your space, do what you need to do to guard yourself from that nonsense.

◄ Allow yourself to be in wonderment and awe of nature, and be open to receiving its profound spiritual lessons about magic and life.

◄ You will gracefully persevere through what may seem like a challenging situation. Believe in yourself, and step up to the challenge.

❀ Puma ❀

Pumas are excellent hunters, who patiently stalk their victims and can jump on average eighteen to twenty feet when attacking their prey. They are principally nocturnal and twilight felines and tend to be loners with what was perceived as a secretive nature. Because of their reputation as fierce hunters, they were associated with military orders in artwork, and curanderx and Mexica warriors were often depicted with puma skins.[247]

At Classic period site Chichen Itza, pumas are prominent in the friezes of jaguars and eagles commemorating the military orders.[248] On a small jadeite pendant from the sacred cenote at Chichen Itza, ruler K'inich Yo'nal Ahk II wears his preinaugural name *kooj*, meaning "puma," on his head. The iconography on this jade piece shows a human head emerging from the mouth of a puma and is similar to that on the headdress of Ruler 3 on Piedras Negras Stela 2.[249] On the pyramid steps at Classic period site Bonampak is a curandero standing between dancers wearing a puma-skin cape, a dark blue oblong headdress, and a simple white oval pectoral ornament visible in front of the knot in the tie around his neck. His gesture and position suggest he is a ritual specialist who directs the ceremonial activities.[250]

Nonordinary Realm Associations: Underworld
Spiritual and Shapeshifting Medicine: stealth, power, bravery, and independence
Symbolism Meanings

◄ Remove yourself from external distractions, and independently reflect on your next steps.

◄ What you have been working toward is almost within your grasp. Be patient, and keep after it.

◄ Do not be afraid to be on your own for a while. You will grow greatly from the experience in various ways.

◄ Step into your role as a leader. There are others who could greatly benefit from your guidance, wisdom, and experience.

❁ Purple Gallinule ❁

The purple gallinule is a waterbird about the size of a dove that has radiant purple-blue plumage that often looks green and turquoise in the sunlight. On the front of its head is a thin row of feathers that create a round light-blue patch that curanderx identified as a divinatory mirror and earned the bird the name "mirror head."[251] Motecuhzoma Xocoyotzin, the ninth *tlatoani*, or ruler, of Tenochtitlan who reigned from 1502 to 1520, saw various bad omens foreshadowing the ominous arrival of the Spaniards. In the seventh omen he saw their arrival depicted on the mirror head of a purple gallinule. The hour was noon, but the night sky with the three stars in the constellation of Taurus could be seen. After the appearance of the stars, he saw strange men on the backs of horses. He took this vision as a bad omen. When he called for the opinion of his sages, the bird disappeared.[252]

Nonordinary Realm Associations: Upperworld, Middleworld, and Underworld

Spiritual and Shapeshifting Medicine: clairvoyance, candor, flashiness, and determination

Symbolism Meanings

◄ Pay attention to any possible signs of upcoming problems and issues. Decide your next course of action wisely, and stay away from any drama.

◄ If you are looking at a situation strictly from the vantage point of who is wrong or right, you are missing the nuances of the situation and the lessons they have to teach you.

◄ Be more conscientious of how you are spending your money. Money is an energy currency that can solidify various kinds of freedom as well as entrapments.

Plate 1. Owl in a temple, bottom left.

From Codex Borgia, Joseph Florimond, duc de Loubat Collection (Loubat 1898), page 18. Courtesy of Ancient Americas at LACMA.

Plate 2. A bat enters the quadrangle with four hummingbirds surrounding and attempting to feed off the bat (top center). The bat is anthropomorphic with a humanlike face.

From Codex Borgia, Joseph Florimond, duc de Loubat Collection (Loubat 1898), page 44. Courtesy of Ancient Americas at LACMA.

Plate 3. The blue road carries Stripe Eye and Xochipilli into the open mouth of the earth caiman, who has long white and red hair, a yellow face, pointed red and white-tipped scales, a yellow body, and a red arc around the eye identifying him as Cipactli. His lips are elongated in the wide toothy maw of the caiman, signaling an entrance into the earth and the Underworld.

From Codex Borgia, Joseph Florimond, duc de Loubat Collection (Loubat 1898), page 39. Courtesy of Ancient Americas at LACMA.

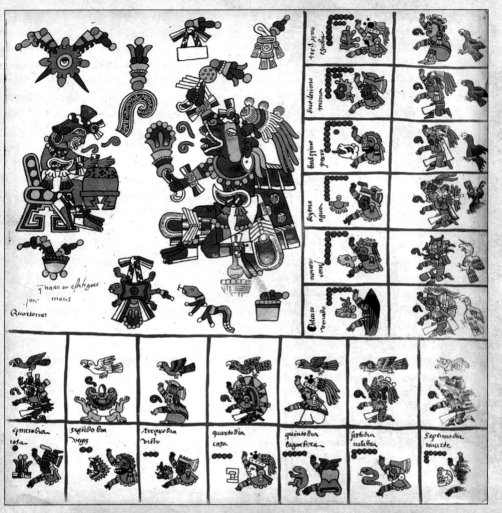

Plate 4. One of the Central Mexican deities, Huehuecoyotl (old coyote).
He is standing on the right of the main top left image with a round gourd rattle
and a flowered baton.

From Codex Borbonicus, Joseph Florimond, duc de Loubat Collection
(Loubat 1899), page 4.
Courtesy of Ancient Americas at LACMA.

Plate 5. Patron of the day sign, lizard. The lizard is on the bottom left with a yellow body and an extended red tongue.

From Codex Borgia, Joseph Florimond, duc de Loubat Collection (Loubat 1898), page 10. Courtesy of Ancient Americas at LACMA.

Plate 6. The quetzal is the second image on the top left row of birds. The macaw is in the middle of the top row.

From Codex Borgia, Joseph Florimond, duc de Loubat Collection (Loubat 1898), page 71. Courtesy of Ancient Americas at LACMA.

Plate 7. Coming from the white cord beginning at the top right and moving left and down are the rabbit as the moon, the deer as the sun, jade, the bent staff of Quetzalcoatl, bloody maguey spines, the white banner of sacrifice, the white down-ball of sacrifice, and a spider at the end.

From Codex Borgia, Joseph Florimond, duc de Loubat Collection (Loubat 1898), page 33. Courtesy of Ancient Americas at LACMA.

In plates 8–11, we see the raccoon in the topmost part of each image utilizing dancing fans, a rattle staff, and belt tinklers to engage in New Year ceremonies, which included honoring the year bearer of that year. There were four year bearers that controlled the fortune of the thirteen years that follow. Each of the four year bearers was oriented to a cardinal space with its own distinct characteristics, divine beings, meanings, and rituals.

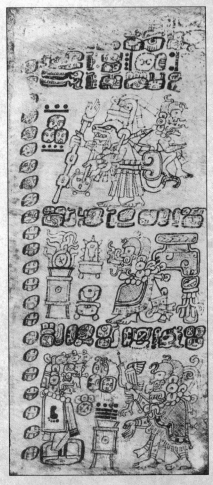

Plate 8. Raccoon is carrying the rain deity, Chaac, on its back.

From Codex Dresdensis,
Ernst Förstemann, page 25.
Courtesy of Ancient Americas at LACMA.

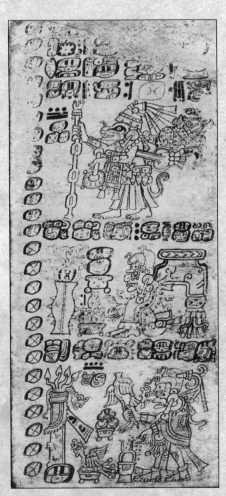

Plate 9. Raccoon appears to be carrying a jaguar on its back on a water lily–type back rack.

From Codex Dresdensis,
Ernst Förstemann, page 26.
Courtesy of Ancient Americas at LACMA.

Plate 10. Raccoon appears to be standing on a crescent moon and is carrying the corn deity on its back rack. This image is likely associated with rituals performed for the year bearer Kan (corn) and the East.

From Codex Dresdensis, Ernst Förstemann, page 27. Courtesy of Ancient Americas at LACMA.

Plate 11. Raccoon appears to be standing on a crescent moon and is carrying the deity of death on his back.

From Codex Dresdensis, Ernst Förstemann, page 28. Courtesy of Ancient Americas at LACMA.

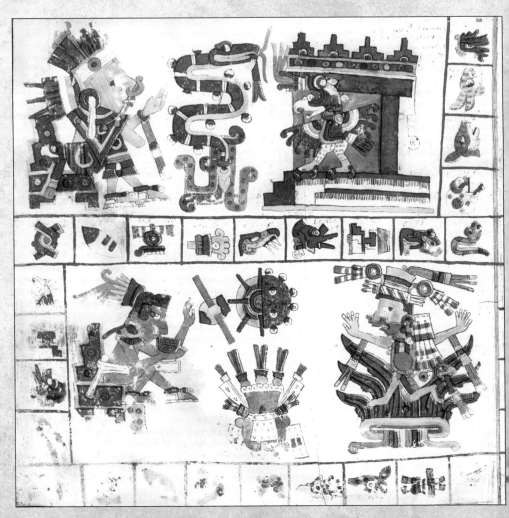

Plate 12. Vulture in the temple, top right.

From Codex Borgia, Joseph Florimond, duc de Loubat Collection (Loubat 1898), page 68.
Courtesy of Ancient Americas at LACMA.

◄ Take inventory of how you are investing your time, what you are doing, and who you are spending your time with. How many of these activities, circumstances, and people nourish and nurture your soul and spirit?

☀ Quetzal ☀

Quetzals were adored and valued for their iridescent green or golden-green wing coverts, backs, chests, and heads; red bellies; and metallic blue upper wings.[253] Males usually have very long green upper-tail coverts, while parts of the females' plumage are brown or grey. Quetzals had great importance in the economy, religion, society, and culture of Mesoamerica. Because they are diurnal birds and tend to come out in the morning, they were often associated with solar and animating soul energy.

The Maya of the northern highlands traded the long quetzal tails of males, which often adorned regal headdresses and sacred objects belonging to rulers and curanderx, including staffs of office, bundles, and bloodletters.[254] The quetzal is the national bird of Guatemala, and Tecun Uman, one of the last rulers of the K'iché' Maya in Guatemala, was believed to have shapeshifted into a quetzal and then an eagle before he was killed in a battle against the Spaniards.

The Central Mexican peoples believed that a way to increase tonalli included dressing in the iridescent green feathers of the quetzal and that the daily path fof the sun was adorned with quetzal feathers.[255] The green feathers of the quetzal were also associated with the renewal of vegetation.[256] Quetzals were often drawn on top of a tree in the eastern quadrant of the cardinal spaces, which is related to fertility, abundance, and wealth.[257]

Nonordinary Realm Associations: Upperworld
Spiritual and Shapeshifting Medicine: majesty, shamanism, prosperity, and leadership

Symbolism Meanings

- ◄ Use your natural magnetism to draw in people and circumstances that will enable you to realize your goals.
- ◄ Develop your shamanic skills and talents to understand yourself on a deeper level.
- ◄ It is time to replenish your sacred animating energies with activities that will nourish your spirit and soul.
- ◄ Make time to engage in morning meditations, breathwork, yoga, or sacred movement; you will find that your day will unfold with greater ease and clarity.

❋ Rabbit ❋

Rabbits are rather fast breeders, are more active around dawn and dusk, and forage primarily at night. Consequently, they were associated with the moon, night sky, Underworld, Middleworld, and the earth's fertility.[258] Most female rabbits become sexually mature at three to eight months of age and can conceive at any time of the year for the duration of their life. After giving birth to four to twelve babies, they can become pregnant again as early as the next day and can deliver up to sixty rabbits a year.

In Classic Maya mythologies, the rabbit was the moon's cohort and typically appeared with lunar Deity I. The rabbit is also somewhat of a trickster and an accomplice in teaching the vain God L, a merchant trader, lessons in humility. On Classic Maya Vase 5359, the Hero Twins stripped Deity L of his fine clothes and flung them into the air, beginning his humiliation and defeat. The moon goddess and her rabbit companion are watching from above. On the Rabbit Vase 1398, Deity L is on his knees submitting to the authority of the sun deity and petitioning for his aid. The rabbit apparently has stolen Deity L's clothes and accoutrements. Unbeknownst to Deity L, the sun deity is working with the rabbit, who is hiding behind the sun deity and has Deity L's goods. On Classic Maya Vase 5166, the rabbit has taken Deity L's clothes and accessories to the moon goddess, and Deity L is kneeling before her, asking for their return.[259] Linguistic evidence from Classic Maya texts suggests that the rabbit represented the face of the moon and was also associated with young children.[260]

The rabbit also appears as a trickster in the Popol Vuh when it helps the Hero Twins by hopping across the playing field like a bouncing ball to divert the attention of the lords of the Underworld when they are playing ball against each other.[261]

In the Legend of the Suns, after fearless Nanahuatzin threw himself into a fiery pit and is resurrected as Tonatiuh, Tecuciztecatl, embarrassed by his own cowardice, threw himself into the fire and rose up. Due to his cowardice, one of the deities threw a rabbit in his face and darkened his shine, and he became the moon.[262] In the Codex Borgia on page 33, a white cord descends from a temple and has attached to it a series of heavenly and religious elements, including the rabbit as the moon (see plate 7).[263]

Rabbit (*tochtli*) was the eighth day sign of the Mexica's tonalpohualli, and was associated with the south. It was a neutral sign and, like the rabbit that could leap in any direction, was somewhat unexpected.[264] The rabbit was largely related to pulque, perhaps in part because rabbits burrow around the roots of the maguey plant.[265]

Nonordinary Realm Associations: Middleworld and Underworld

Spiritual and Shapeshifting Medicine: prosperity, fertility, craftiness, and seduction

Symbolism Meanings

- ◄ Growth spurts in areas of your trade are ripe right now; take advantage of them, and take action.
- ◄ Be mindful of who you align yourself with, and be discerning of anyone that is demanding or expecting you to take sides.
- ◄ Expand your vision. Prosperity will take place in different areas and ways. Refrain from placing all of your goals or vision in one venture or idea.

◄ If you sense that someone or something is potentially harmful to you, leave as quickly as possible.

✾ Raccoon ✾

Raccoons are nocturnal mammals, and they had a reputation for being intelligent and mischievous. Their incredibly dexterous front paws that allow them to readily grab items and their facial markings that look like a mask were likely to blame for their mischievous reputation. The Central Mexicans identified the raccoon as *mapachitli*, or "one who takes everything it sees," and considered it a great thief.[266]

In the Dresden Codex raccoons were metaphors for the dying and reviving year. The upper portion of the New Year passage appearing on Dresden Codex pages 25 to 28 features a raccoon depicted as a dancer, with rattle staffs, dancing fans, and belt tinklers (see plates 8–11). The raccoon actors are engaging in a ceremony and perhaps also shaping the prognostications for the incoming year. Four raccoons are shown, each one bearing a scepter in a hand: one carries a god of rain, another carries a jaguar, another carries a god of corn, and the final one carries a god of death. These four raccoons are likely representations of the four gods who hold up the sky, known as the *bacabs,* or *chacs,* associated with the New Year festivals celebrated among the Yucatec Maya during the *wayeb'** and the first day of the following year.[267]

Nonordinary Realm Associations: Middleworld and Underworld
Spiritual and Shapeshifting Medicine: adaptability, intelligence, shrewdness, and magic
Symbolism Meanings
  ◄ Be discreet in your new plans. There is some unwanted energy you should consider avoiding.

---

*The Maya Solar Haab' calendar was made up of eighteen months of twenty days with five "nameless days" known as wayeb' at the end of the year.

◄ In making plans for any new ventures, refrain from placing all of your eggs in one basket. Diversify a little bit more, and see which plans bloom and which ones you enjoy; then determine your next steps.

◄ Do not wait for someone to give you an opportunity to do what you love. Take life by the reins, and create opportunities for yourself.

◄ Make sure you are well taken care of and remember to also make time to help and be considerate of others.

❈ Rat ❈

Rats are medium-sized, long-tailed rodents that have a keen sense of smell and are easy to train. They are generally very adaptable and are found living alongside humans in the walls and in in-between spaces. They become sexually mature at five to six weeks of age and are generally very fertile. The brown female rat, for example, can breed throughout the year with up to five litters a year and fourteen babies per litter. Perhaps due to their adaptability and trainability, they were often seen as helpers and servers of the lords of the Underworld.[268]

Like mice, they were also privy to confidential information. In the Popol Vuh, a rat tells the Hero Twins of their fathers' gaming tools, which their grandmother was hiding above the house. It was the gaming tools that awakened the lords of the Underworld and caused them to demand the presence of their fathers, One Hunahpu and Seven Hunahpu, who died in the Underworld.[269]

Nonordinary Realm Associations: Middleworld and Underworld
Spiritual and Shapeshifting Medicine: resilience, eavesdropping, fecundity, and pliability
Symbolism Meanings

◄ You can get through anything. You are an incredible survivor and very resourceful; do not forget this.

◄ Be courageous and brave in pursuing your goals, but make

sure you are not being reckless. Carefully study and assess your circumstances before taking action.

◄ You have innate intuitive gifts. Trust your intuition in determining other people's prerogatives and whom to align yourself with.

◄ Abundance is on the horizon. Be more assertive in obtaining it.

✻ Ringtail ✻

The bodies of ringtails resemble cats, but they have a pointed muzzle with long whiskers and a long black-and-white ringed tail of fourteen to sixteen stripes. They are nocturnal with short, straight, semiretractable claws, allowing them to climb and hunt small prey. They are omnivores with a great sense of smell. They were known for being very clever and worked together. At night they would cry out to lure small dogs and were known for preying on them.[270]

Nonordinary Realm Associations: Underworld
Spiritual and Shapeshifting Medicine: playfulness, cunning, stealth, and astuteness
Symbolism Meanings

◄ Work your charm and charisma to attract what you are seeking.

◄ You will have a better chance of realizing your goals, if you make yourself aware of other people's strengths and utilize them by working together.

◄ Do not take yourself so seriously; be sure to make time and space to be silly and playful.

◄ You have a knack for influencing others through speech. Continue to develop these communication skills and take them to another level.

✻ Scorpion ✻

Scorpions are incredibly resilient, nocturnal, predatory arachnids that find shelter during the day in underground holes or underneath rocks and brush. They can go an entire year without eating due to the large amount of food they can consume when they eat, the efficient way their bodies handle the nutrition, and their ability to slow their metabolism. Their large claws are studded with highly sensitive tactile hair, which they use to catch their prey. Depending on the toxicity of their venom and size of their claws, they will either crush the prey or inject it with neurotoxic venom in order to eat it. In ancient Mesoamerica, their stinger was often assigned virile phallic associations. They were also associated with celestial night imagery, agricultural, and rain-related themes and were often used to make offerings and medicine.

In Classic Maya art, there was sometimes a fusion of the scorpion with the maize deity, perhaps indicative of a prosperous period of rain and agriculture.[271] The celestial imagery was often contentious. In the Ritual of the Bacabs, the scorpion was depicted as an eclipse demon.[272] Scorpions were also associated with Venus and the Scorpius constellation. The Colonial period dictionaries from the Yucatán identify *zinaan ek* (scorpion stars) as the sign of Scorpio, and the Chilam Balam books also list the "black scorpion" among the stellar deities involved in the *katun* prophecies. At Chichen Itza, the lintel of the eastern doorway of the nunnery (observatory) depicts a text that shows a celestial scorpion. Scorpion traits may be seen on a skeletal snake representing Scorpius that may be equated with the War Serpent.[273]

The Central Mexicans used scorpions as offerings and likely the *Megacormus gertschi* scorpion (a.k.a., the Mexican scorpion) as medicine. While most scorpion venom components are peptidic or proteinic

in nature, the alkaloid of the Mexican scorpion has medicinal properties as well. Burned scorpions were used in ointment as an offering to their deities and to cure the sick and little children.[274] There is also a myth wherein the lunar-earth deity, Xochiquetzal, seduced her pious brother, who was later punished by losing his head and being transformed into a scorpion.[275]

Nonordinary Realm Associations: Underworld

Spiritual and Shapeshifting Medicine: strength, defensiveness, adaptability, and prudence

Symbolism Meanings

- ◄ While you are incredibly resilient, make sure you refrain from isolating yourself for extended periods of time.
- ◄ There is a situation you need to be more discerning about; not everything is as it appears. Trust your intuition, even if your rational mind is convincing you of something else. Pay attention.
- ◄ Take some time out for yourself regularly to do nothing but rest and recharge.
- ◄ Make sure you are saving and investing toward more financial freedom.

☀ Shark ☀

Sharks can swim as fast as twelve miles per hour when hunting, and some, such as the shortfin mako, can burst up to thirty-one miles per hour. Sharks have excellent hearing and a keen sense of smell, and their use of sight likely varies with species and water conditions. They often symbolized the dreaded aspects of the Underworld, and a shark diadem likely related to warfare and bloodletting rites.[296] The edges of the teeth from certain sharks, such as the tiger shark and great blue shark, are serrated and were presumably used for bloodletting rites.[297]

The *xoc* shark glyph and spondylus shell were often worn together as a belt ornament by the maize deity probably to illustrate the deity giving birth to new maize and thus renewing the cycle of earthly fertility. The belt seems to have also represented counting missed days of blood menstruation during pregnancy; a sacrifice performed by women to renew the human cycle of life.[298]

Xoc, a malignant Underworld deity, was known to devour people and animals.[299] The bull shark was likely the prime candidate for this Underworld deity, as it can travel up rivers to freshwater inland lakes and had encounters with the lowland Maya.[300]

Nonordinary Realm Associations: Underworld

Spiritual and Shapeshifting Medicine: fearlessness, intuition, grace, and stealth

Symbolism Meanings

◄ Do not let fear hold you back from what your heart desires; go after it full speed ahead.

◄ There is true strength in allowing ourselves to show our deep emotions and be vulnerable. At the same time, there is profound wisdom in knowing whom we can allow ourselves to be vulnerable with. Make sure you are keeping both in mind and heart.

◄ Follow your intuition as to what you feel is right for you.

◄ Pay attention to how you feel after eating particular foods, and honor your body.

✺ Skunk ✺

Skunks are principally nocturnal and have strong front claws for digging, excellent hearing, and a great sense of smell, but they have poor vision. During the day, they generally burrow underground. They refrain from spraying their pungent unpleasant scent that is somewhat difficult to wash off, as they carry just enough of the chemical for five or six uses, and it takes about ten days to produce another supply. Because of this unpleasant odor, predatorial animals tend to leave them alone. The Central Mexican deity Tezcatlipoca commonly shapeshifted into skunks, which were also associated with Tezcatlipoca's farts.[293] According to the Codex Badiano, skunk blood, along with plumerias, cacao flowers, rainwater, bay leaf, and a few other ingredients, was used to treat heightened anxiety and fear.[294] If someone had a dream of a skunk entering a home or giving birth inside their home, it was believed that the owner of the home would die soon, or another bad event would take place.[295]

Nonordinary Realm Associations: Underworld

Spiritual and Shapeshifting Medicine: balance, discernment, awareness, and assertiveness

Symbolism Meanings

- ◄ Know your boundaries. Express them clearly when needed, and when they are not respected, step away from the person or circumstances that are not respecting them.
- ◄ Believe in yourself, and do not be afraid to stand up for yourself and express what you need.
- ◄ Even if you cannot see what is to come, assess what you know about all the circumstances, weigh the pros and cons, and trust your judgment.
- ◄ Have you been pushing people away? Take some time to calmly reflect as to whether you need to balance and check your ego.

❁ Snail (Queen Conch) ❁

The queen conch is one of the largest marine snails. Adult shells, which are solid and heavy and have nine to eleven whorls and a widely flaring and thickened outer lip, were used as trumpets in various kinds of ceremonies and were often incised with the name of the user or the ancestors being called forth.[301]

Conchs were largely associated with fertility, life, wind, animating essence energy, and creation.[302] The Maya used them to communicate with supernatural beings and ancestors during bloodletting rites. At

San Bartolo, animating soul energy is depicted as a shell air volute coming out of a mouth. In their manuscripts, the spiral shell also served as a numeral sign as the glyph for zero.[303]

Central Mexican wind deity, Ehecatl-Quetzalcoatl, and his animal coessence, Xolotl, were both depicted with a cut-conch shell pendant.[304] In the Legend of the Suns, Quetzalcoatl as a challenge from Mictlantecuhtli blows music from a solid conch shell with the help of bees and earthworms. Afterward, Mictlantecuhtli gave him the bones of humans from the previous world.[305]

Nonordinary Realm Associations: Underworld

Spiritual and Shapeshifting Medicine: shamanic insights, power, revival, and leadership

Symbolism Meanings

- ◄ Consider taking curanderismo/shamanic classes and developing your skills to journey into nonordinary realms.
- ◄ Step into and claim your abilities and gifts to lead others in ways that feel good to you.
- ◄ It is time to clearly define your boundaries and speak your truth, especially with people that you feel are not honoring you.
- ◄ Invest time and engage in activities that will allow you to rest, reflect on your next steps, and rejuvenate.

❂ Snake ❂

Some snakes live underground, others can swim in water or slither up trees, and all of them use their sense of smell to track their prey via their forked tongues, which are in constant motion collecting airborne particles that give them a sense of smell and taste simultaneously. Snakes were believed to be able to move between and serve as conduits for the nonordinary realms, and ancestors and deities were often depicted as coming out of the mouth of snake-type beings, who facilitated communication and passage into these realms.[276] They also often had regenerative associations, likely due to the molting of their skin: young snakes can shed their skin every two weeks, and older snakes can shed their skin two to four times a year, depending on their size and species. This regenerative association linked them to life-giving earth energy that produces new growth. Snakes also had fertility associations, with their bodies correlating with penises and their mouths with vaginas.[277]

Their undulating bodies often symbolized water and lightning, and deities foretelling coming rain or principal rain deities were depicted wielding snakes as staffs or headdresses. Snakes also had celestial links. The body of the two-headed snake was often conceived as a sky band that represented the Milky Way and the ecliptic, the celestial path of the sun, moon, and planets.[278]

The principal Maya rain deity, also known as Chaac, often wielded snakes and axes as symbols of lightning. Lightning was also depicted as a fire serpent and the lightning axe that could be conflated as a single object.[279] Lunar earth deity Goddess O was often depicted with a snake headdress, which had associations with storms and water.[280]

Maya rulers and the royal court often impersonated the Water Lily Serpent, linking them to not only physical control over water sources but also to supernatural control over these tangible elements. On Stela C of Classic period site Copan, the ruler 18 Rabbit was depicted grasping a double-headed snake bar, demonstrating his ability to wield this bar to invoke ancestors and supernatural beings from the nonordinary realms.[281]

In the Classic period Birth Vase, a group of old midwives with jaguar ears attend a young pregnant woman who is in labor. Her offspring are born from the open maws of two snakes that glide through the mouth of the personified mountain.[282] Snake dances were also performed, perhaps to invoke ancestors or other supernatural beings. The lintels from Classic period site Yaxchilan, for example, depict a snake dance, wherein the dancers hold a snake in their hands, and the position of their inverted feet with ankle lifted signified dancing. One of the texts explains that Bird Jaguar IV is dancing with the sky snake.[283] The Postclassic death deity, Deity A, who had a division sign on his cheek and blackened region around his eye, was often depicted coming out of the jaws of a snake and seems to have been impersonated during ritual theatrical performances.[284]

The Central Mexican rain deity, Tlaloc, was frequently depicted with fire/lightning snakes.[285] Snakes, in their association with penises, were shown coming out of and between third-gender star deities, the Tzitzimime (plural of Tzitzimitl). Snakes also slither under and out of the skirt of lunar earth deity Coatlique, possibly overlapping with beliefs in mythical dangerous toothed vaginas.[286] The coral snake, in particular, was often paired with female deities in codices and tied around or came out of their lower extremities.[287] Serpent (coatl) was the fifth day sign of the Mexica's tonalpohualli and was associated with the east. Those born on this day were destined to be paupers and live financially menial lives, imitating snakes who went about homeless and naked, exposed to the sun and the wind, living in one hole one day and in another the next day.[288] It was also a bad omen to have certain species of snakes cross one's path. People believed, for example, that if a viper crossed one's path, death or disease would ensue.[289] Because of their fertility connections, potions were also made from snakes to increase sexual performance.[290]

In Central Mexico, the rattlesnake was called the "yellow lord" because it was believed to be the leader of snakes.[291] Rattlesnakes, in particular, were considered vision serpents, or conduits to nonordinary realms. They also symbolized the Pleiades *(tzab)*. The tzab also served as a special insignia for curanderx who carried a short stick with a rattlesnake's tail attached to it.[292]

Nonordinary Realm Associations: Upperworld, Middleworld, and Underworld

Spiritual and Shapeshifting Medicine: transformation, irrepressibility, psychic nature, and rebirth

Symbolism Meanings

◄ Let go of identities and stories that are weighing you down.

Understand that they have power over you because you allow this. Create new ones that will allow you to flow more gracefully on your current path.

◄ Let yourself stay calm and centered amid change, especially when it feels or seems chaotic. This will allow you to continue to change with ease and grace.

◄ Take the time and energy to adequately assess the benefits and possible disadvantages of investing in any new ventures, rather than simply diving in.

◄ If you would like to connect more with ancestral medicine, guidance, and wisdom, accept and know that you have always been connected to your ancestors. Work on clearing feelings of separation or of being disconnected from them, instead of "trying" to connect with them; trying presumes separation. There is no trying; there is only accepting and knowing that you have always been connected to your ancestors and their medicine, wisdom, and guidance.

☀ Sparrow Hawk ☀

Sparrow hawks are small, broad-winged diurnal raptors with long tails; long, thin yellow legs; and talons they use for catching other smaller birds. Females tend to be up to 25 percent larger than males. During breeding, males tend to do all the hunting for both their young and the mother until the chicks are old enough to be left alone. Afterward both parents hunt for the juveniles and continue to do so for up to about a month, when their young have left the nest. The Central Mexicans called sparrow hawks "frost callers," because they were believed to announce the approach of the cold season. Their cries were identified as bad omens among traveling tradespeople.[309]

Nonordinary Realm Associations: Upperworld
Spiritual and Shapeshifting Medicine: warrior, perception, aggression, and tenacity

Symbolism Meanings

◄ You are much stronger than you give yourself credit for.

◄ Pay attention. Do not disregard people or circumstances because they appear trivial. Be discerning, and do not allow yourself to become too predictable.

◄ Envision and step into your role as a warrior. Help those that are less privileged and those who are willing to step up and help others as well. Create more leaders.

◄ Consider enrolling in a martial art or some other activity that will inspire you to tap into your internal power in a centered and balanced manner.

❂ Spider ❂

Most spiders are nocturnal and are generally regarded as predators that capture their prey through their sticky webs. In Mesoamerican myths, spiders were widely associated with weaving. They wove passageways from the celestial realms into other realms and were thought to have taught the first women to weave. They were often considered symbols of balance and creation,[310] since the act of weaving was viewed as a means by which the cosmos and the order and continuity of social life was ritually and materially enacted.[311] Many of the earth lunar deities were associated with weaving or spiders.

The Maya deity, Deity N, a quadripartite deity of the four cardinal spaces who was likely associated with and responsible for holding up the four corners of the sky, is sometimes depicted as a spider or coming from a web.[312] In the Tepeu I vessel, Deity N is depicted as a spider balancing the sun and moon and exhaling animating soul energy.[313] The diving stones of the Yucatec Maya curers were called *am*, their word for spider. These stones were used by curanderx to map out the four perimeter points, or cardinal spaces, and to open their portals.[314] During the early Colonial period, Ix Chel was also closely identified with the spider and the am divining stones. In the Ritual of the Bacabs, Ix Chel is identified as a spider, a divining stone, and an aged grandmother.[315]

On page 33 of the Codex Borgia, at the end of the white cord coming from a temple there are various heavenly and religious elements, including a spider (see plate 7).[316] The earth lunar deity Cihuacoatl, as the skeletal Tzitzimime, is sometimes depicted with a spider in her headdress. The Tzitzimime were often represented as spider sky bearers who descended on the world during eclipses and calendrical period endings to wreak havoc on the earth.[317] Spiders were also powerful omens of illness. If a spider entered a house or crossed someone's path, it could signify that someone sent an illness their way or intended to shame them. Upon finding the spider, a person would make two lines on the floor in the form of a cross and then spit out pulque on the middle point and say an invocation to clear away misfortunes.[318]

Nonordinary Realm Associations: Upperworld, Middleworld, and Underworld

Spiritual and Shapeshifting Medicine: creativity, equanimity, prophecy, and resourcefulness

Symbolism Meanings

- ◄ Expand out of your comfort zone, and create new possibilities, connections, and ventures for yourself.
- ◄ Approach any new venture by assessing the terrain and then creating a balanced support system.
- ◄ Maintain a positive vision while you take action to manifest ideal circumstances.
- ◄ In approaching any divinatory activity, remember that you have the right to create your reality. Divination provides insight to a reality that can be shifted.

❂ Spondylus (Spiny Oyster) ❂

Spondylus is a genus of bivalve mollusks that have multiple eyes around the edges of their mantle and well-developed nervous systems. They were associated with ancestors and provided a means for ritual communication and connection to the primordial waters of the Underworld. They were also perceived as symbols of water and fertility and the female womb.[306] Maya rulers were often portrayed with spondylus necklaces, possibly demonstrating their abilities to create and be connected to the nonordinary realms, as well as their ancestors.[307]

Both Atlantic and Pacific species of spondylus have been found in Maya burials as containers for precious objects. The Maya practice of placing spondylus shells over the heads and bodies of the dead parallels the practice of placing a jade bead over their mouths. These shells were likely linked to watery places or watery surfaces that in some way facilitated the rebirth and resurrection of the soul, an appropriate parallel to the rebirth of the sun in the eastern sea.[308]

Nonordinary Realm Associations: Underworld
Spiritual and Shapeshifting Medicine: rebirth, animating soul energy, portals, and new beginnings
Symbolism Meanings

◄ Engage in limpia ceremonies to connect you with your ancestors. They have guidance, medicine, and wisdom for you. This ceremony can include a *velacion* (candle magic) with marigolds as offerings and a petition for their guidance and support.

◄ It is time to open up to new ways of creating and bringing in abundance. The time is ripe to explore new possibilities.

◄ Engage in self-care and self-love practices to revitalize and renew your energy levels and emotional and mental well-being.

◄ Consider going to a body of water and doing some meditative soul searching. The water will calm, center, and ground you, as well as give you greater emotional balance.

❊ Squirrel ❊

Squirrels are small- to medium-sized slender rodents with bushy tails, strong claws for grasping and climbing, and excellent vision. They are incredibly agile and fast and can jump great distances from the ground, averaging four to six feet and farther if they have a running start. They are predominantly herbivorous, but some eat insects and small verte-brates. They were generally identified as being fearless and crafty. They were known by the Central Mexicans as a *techalotl*, or thief, that appeared in plain sight and would steal their food.[319] In the Central Mexican Codex Magliabechiano, the squirrel was the glyph for one of the dance deities who appears as a companion or another form of Ixtlilton, a deity of medicine and healing.[320] The Maya also held them in high regard. A well-known ruler of Naranjo, Guatemala, was "Smoking Squirrel."[321]

Nonordinary Realm Associations: Upperworld and Middleworld

Spiritual and Shapeshifting Medicine: agility, adaptability, rugged-ness, and fearlessness

Symbolism Meanings

- ◄ Be fearless and relentless in pursuing your goals. If you are having difficulty, do not change your goals; change your game plan.
- ◄ Apply your resourcefulness in all areas of your life, and let yourself be flexible when necessary.
- ◄ Observe and assess your surroundings. Once you feel you have a solid understanding of the terrain, set your plans into motion.
- ◄ Remember to take time to play and enjoy your life. Do not take yourself too seriously.

❈ Stingray ❈

Stingrays are typically inactive sea rays that spend the majority of the time partially buried in and camouflaged by the sand. Their flat bodies allow them to effectively conceal themselves, and their sense of smell and electroreceptors allow them to sense the natural electrical charges of potential prey as it swims by. While most stingrays are docile, certain larger species can be more aggressive, and they use their venomous tail spines to attack or defend themselves. Both sides of their whiplike tails, which can be as long as seventeen inches in some species, are lined with sawlike serrations pointing toward the tip.

Stingray spines were used for ritual bloodletting to invoke and communicate with gods or ancestors. They were a common motif in Classic Maya art,[322] and actual stingray spines and replicas in jade and other materials were found in tombs and were often placed in the pelvic area of men.[323]

Nonordinary Realm Associations: Underworld

Spiritual and Shapeshifting Medicine: calm, passivity, concealment, and flexibility

Symbolism Meanings

◄ Take a step back, remain quiet and unnoticed, and observe your environment. You will obtain a better understanding of it.

◄ Make sure you are not forcing yourself on others by always placing yourself in the limelight. Learn to share the spotlight with others.

◄ Keep your goals and plans to yourself. While your friends may ultimately be happy for you, they may initially be slightly envious, and that is energy that should always be avoided when possible.

◄ Give yourself time to process and release any volatile emotions in a safe and peaceful space, and allow yourself to regain equanimity.

☀ Tapir ☀

Tapirs are large herbivorous mammals that are about six feet long and three feet high and can weigh anywhere from 330 to 700 pounds. They resemble pigs, have a short prehensile nose trunk, and are generally passive. They inhabit jungle and forest regions near mud pits or freshwater sources and swim and submerge themselves in water, allowing small fish to pick parasites off their bulky bodies. The Maya associated them with the nocturnal and aquatic creatures of the Underworld.[324]

Tapirs are primarily nocturnal and have voracious appetites for their vegetarian diets. They were very difficult to hunt and kill, largely because of the thick skin on the backs of their necks and their ability to run quite fast. Sahagún reports that even if they were shot with an arrow they could not be killed. In order to capture them hunters would make them fall into a pit and then spear them.[325] In many myths, they were seducers of women, likely due to their particularly large genitalia.[326]

Nonordinary Realm Associations: Middleworld and Underworld

Spiritual and Shapeshifting Medicine: imperviousness, spiritedness, swiftness, and toughness

Symbolism Meanings

- ◄ Develop a thick skin, and don't be concerned with what others say or think about you.
- ◄ Let yourself roam free, and discover what makes you happy and satisfies your spirit and soul.
- ◄ Your spirit is resilient and playful; allow these amazing characteristics about yourself to shine.
- ◄ Be gentle and patient with yourself, and give yourself time to rest and revitalize.

❂ Toad ❂

Toads were associated with transformation, likely due to their life cycle, in which most of them change from an egg to a tadpole and then to a four-legged carnivorous animal. They also shed and consume their own skin several times a year. They can lay thousands of eggs in a year, which also linked them to fertility and the Middleworld.[330] Because they give birth in watery environments, and the moon controls the tides and all bodies of water, toads were also connected to water and the moon[331] and associated with the Central Mexican rain deity, Tlaloc.[332]

Toads have a pair of parotoid glands on the back of their heads that contain an alkaloid poison that they excrete when stressed. The excreted poison can differ depending on the toad. The Sonoran Desert toad, for example, excretes a psychoactive bufotoxin. To experience the psychoactive effects, the back of the toad could be licked. Maya curanderx also added this psychoactive to their brew of tobacco to increase its intoxicating properties.[333] It is likely that Maya Classic vessel 3 depicts a sitting Sonoran Desert toad with a lily* on its forehead, and Deity C, who represented the essence of sacrality, on its back.[334] The psychoactive effects of the toxin this toad excreted were most likely identified as being sacred.

Something or someone emerging out of a toad's mouth signified a rebirth or new beginning. In Maya Classic period stucco reliefs adorning Balamku's Casa de los Cuatro Reyes, the four figures found on the roof of the building's superstructure each depict a ruler emerging from the mouth of a toad, which itself sits on a cleft mountain. This mountain is a register of aquatic imagery suggesting a time before or just at the moment of creation. The use of toad imagery to signal rebirth or sprouting is found in the logographic sign for birth, which is a toad head.[335] In addition, the uinal glyph for twenty days was a toad, which signaled a rebirth of a new period of twenty days.

Nonordinary Realm Associations: Middleworld and Underworld
Spiritual and Shapeshifting Medicine: fecundity, transformation, clairvoyance, and renewal
Symbolism Meanings
- ◄ Engage in trance journeys to help you to further understand and define your happiness and passion.
- ◄ While unexpected changes are on the horizon, you can still prepare yourself by being open to flow and dynamically integrate these changes.
- ◄ Consider taking up meditative movement practices, such as qigong, and let yourself experience the subtle natural energies all around you to better understand your own.
- ◄ Continue to develop your intuitive skills and abilities to further your connection with the nonordinary realms.

---

*White lilies have a calming and mild sedative effect and are believed to have been placed in the inebriating balche drink of the Maya, so it is not surprising that the toad with an image of Deity C is fashioning a white lily on its forehead.

❀ Turkey ❀

Turkeys are one of the largest birds in their ranges. Male turkeys have a distinctive fleshy wattle called a snood that hangs from the top of the beak. Males with longer snoods are deferred to, and females prefer to mate with them. The Central Mexicans believed that feeding the snood to men could cause impotence.[327] Turkeys were considered animals that commoners born on Ce Ehecatl could shapeshift into.[328] The Maya kept ocellated turkeys in pens as pets. They also offered turkeys at New Year ceremonies to ensure a prosperous and fortunate upcoming year. In the Maya Madrid Codex, turkeys were depicted tied to world trees, signaling this tradition.[329]

Nonordinary Realm Associations: Middleworld
Spiritual and Shapeshifting Medicine: fertility, abundance, generosity, and gregariousness
Symbolism Meanings
- Pathways are being cleared for your overall prosperity and good fortune.
- Be open to receiving generosity, love, and praise. You deserve it and are completely worth it.
- Explore new ways to bring abundance into your life and diversify these resources.
- Take time to connect with nature and the earth and her cycles. Consider going hiking or camping more often.

❀ Turtle (Tortoise) ❀

Turtles* are reptiles of the order Testudines that have a cartilaginous shell or carapace developed from their ribs that acts as a shield. Turtles, including aquatic ones, breathe air and must surface at regular inter-

---

*The term *turtle* is used to describe all species of this order, regardless of whether they are land dwelling or water dwelling, whereas the term *tortoise* is used strictly for slow-moving terrestrial species.

vals to refill their lungs. Even though many species live in or around water, they do not lay eggs underwater. Sea turtles, for example, lay eggs on sandy beaches. Turtles are generally shy, hide in their carapace, and move rather slowly. Turtles were often seen as symbols of the earth's surface, water, and sky beings.[336]

The theme of the Maya maize deity emerging out of a turtle's carapace as the earth is recurring in Classic Maya art.[337] Turtle shells were struck like a drum with a stick or an antler and were considered the earth lord's musical instrument.[338] An aspect of Deity N, the quadripartite deity, may be a deity of thunder. Deity N is often depicted in a turtle carapace, and the ritual instrumental sounds made from playing the turtle shell were used to imitate the sound of thunder.[339]

Turtle imagery was also reflected in the night sky in the turtle constellation that corresponded to the belt of the Western constellation Orion, which could be observed at midnight on the ending of a katun and was marked by three T510b star glyphs.[340]

Nonordinary Realm Associations: Middleworld and Underworld

Spiritual and Shapeshifting Medicine: abundance, change, intuition, and rebirth

Symbolism Meanings

- ◂ Do not become discouraged if your hopes and dreams have not come to fruition. Continue to move forward with discernment, persistence, and resolve.

- ◂ Always approach your path with compassion, patience, love, and tenderness.

- ◂ Let go of expectations, and do not be in a rush to get to what you perceive as the finish line. Enjoy the process because it encompasses the majority of our experiences in life.

- ◂ Make sure you finish what you started, even if it looks very different from what you first imagined.

❀ Vulture ❀

Vultures are scavenging birds of prey who eat mainly dead animals, but they may kill live prey if it is wounded or ill. Despite the fact that they do not have normal feathers on their heads, aerodynamically they are the best of the soaring land birds, riding majestically on air currents. They help keep humans healthy by cleansing the earth of rotting flesh and excrement and consuming and removing bacteria that would be potentially lethal.[341]

Vultures were associated with solar and celestial bodies, symbolized death and disease, and were depicted in codices as attacking humans.[342] In various Maya mythologies, the vulture, particularly the king vulture, is identified as the sun's adversary, either as a rival for the moon's affection or as the Principal Bird Deity, who has vulture traits and poses as the false sun.[343] In the Popol Vuh, the Principal Bird Deity is the egotistical Seven Macaw, who obscured the light of the sun and moon and demanded to be adored for the brilliant shine in the gold, silver, and jewels in his eyes and teeth. The Hero Twins saw the evil in his pride and decided to bring him down. Hunahpu, one of the Hero Twins, took out one of Seven Macaw's teeth with his blowgun. The twins were also aided by humble healer grandparents who tricked Seven Macaw into releasing all of the gold, silver, and jewels from his teeth and eyes, which ultimately led to his downfall.[344]

The turkey vulture (*cozcacuauhtli*) was the sixteenth day sign of the Mexica's tonalpohualli and was associated with the south. Those born under this day sign were known to give good counsel and were fond of gathering and instructing disciples.[345] They were also the representatives of the Cihuateteo, the spirits of women who had died while giving birth and had become gods.[346]

Nonordinary Realm Associations: Upperworld, Middleworld, and Underworld

Spiritual and Shapeshifting Medicine: metamorphosis, purification, restoration, and resourcefulness

Symbolism Meanings

- ◄ The coming change that is inevitable will inspire you to grow in unprecedented ways. Trust that the universe is always conspiring for your benefit.

- ◄ You may feel challenged right now, but these feelings ultimately stem from doubting yourself. Put effort into meeting the challenge, and excel. You've got this!

- ◄ Stop making excuses, and let go of people and circumstances that are toxic or are weighing you down.

- ◄ Show gratitude to those who have been loyal and loving to you and continue to inspire them as they inspire you.

❁ Water Turkey ❁

Water turkeys are large waterbirds that hunt by stretching out their necks and spearing fish and other small prey with their sharp, slender beaks. Unlike other waterbirds, water turkeys do not have waterproof feathers and as a result cannot stay floating on water for long periods of time. Their dense bones, wetted plumage, and neutral buoyancy in water allow them to fully submerge and search for prey underwater. They were considered next in hierarchy after the pelican, likely due to their adept hunting skills. The Central Mexicans considered them the heart of the water and a leader of the waterbirds, because they mirrored many traits of the pelican.[347]

Nonordinary Realm Associations: Upperworld, Middleworld, and Underworld

Spiritual and Shapeshifting Medicine: boldness, precision, versatility, and persistence

Symbolism Meanings

- ◄ Invest time in mastering a new talent or skill, and integrate it into your role as a leader or teacher.

- Take some time for yourself to do some introspective soul-searching and reflect on where you are at and how you want to keep growing.
- Be clear and precise as to what you want, and do not let anything distract you from realizing your goals.
- You have the impetus and precision to direct your vision and put it into action. Use this space and time to do just that.

❀ Weasel ❀

Weasels are stealthy nocturnal carnivorous predators with short legs and long, slender bodies, which enable them to follow their prey—principally rats, mice, voles, and rabbits—into burrows. Because their bodies do not store fat, they need a constant supply of food to provide energy, so they spend most of their time hunting. Before killing their prey, they bob back and forth and hop in a dance, which is meant to intimidate the other animal. Thereafter, they force themselves on their prey.[348] In the Popol Vuh, one of the dances the Hero Twins performed for the lords of the Underworld before their defeat was the weasel dance.[349]

The Central Mexicans identified weasels as war captains and messengers boding illness and death.[350] Commoners born on Ce Ehecatl are able to shapeshift into weasels.[351] When someone dreamed of a weasel crossing the path in front of them, it was said that they would have difficulty going where they wanted to go and could be led astray.[352]

Nonordinary Realm Associations: Underworld
Spiritual and Shapeshifting Medicine: action, ritual dance, stealth, and undetectability
Symbolism Meanings
- Keep your intentions and plans largely to yourself. Let only those people who are essential to your plans' materialization in on them.
- When considering new ventures in which to invest your time and money, be diligent in your search, and do not cut corners.

◄ Trust your perception, and listen to your intuition. It is imperative that you approach this next phase from this space, rather than simply relying on your mental faculties.

◄ It is time for a holistic cleanse of physical, emotional, spiritual, and mental toxins.

◉ Western Grebe ◉

Western grebes are slender waterbirds with red eyes, long necks, small heads, and long-pointed bills. They are social birds and nest in colonies of hundreds, principally on large inland lakes and marshes. They are known for their distinct communication calls, such as making ticking noises to warn their young of danger, and their dramatic courtship display in which two or more race side by side across the water, their necks gracefully curved and bills pointed to the sky. They are almost always resting on the surface of the water or diving for prey for what can be extended periods of time. They were known to sing just before sunrise, and when they did, other waterfowl would answer them, announcing the coming of dawn.[353]

Nonordinary Realm Associations: Upperworld, Middleworld, and Underworld

Spiritual and Shapeshifting Medicine: vocalization, sociability, romance, and loyalty

Symbolism Meanings

◄ This is a time to be more social. Strike up conversations with new people, and expand your circle of friends.

◄ Pay attention; a pathway is opening for a new beginning. See if it is something that aligns with you.

◄ If you are questioning whether you should remain in a relationship, especially a romantic one, ask yourself, "Does it pretty much flow with grace?" If it does not, then work on your authentic self-worth and self-love, and then ask yourself whether you deserve a graceful, loving, supportive relationship.

◄ If you sense that something is not right, speak up and do something about it.

☀ West Mexican Black Bear ☀

The Mexican black is a subspecies of the American black bear and is native to north-central and northeastern Mexico, respectively. They are the smallest bear species, and because they are omnivores, their diets largely depend on the season and location. They are highly dexterous, have immense physical strength, and can run as fast as twenty-five to thirty miles per hour. They are generally adept climbers and swimmers and have a keen sense of smell, excellent memory, and better hearing and vision than most humans. They use shelters, such as caves and logs, as their dens to hibernate during the winter and are generally solitary, except when the young are with their mothers. Sahagún identifies these bears as *cuetlachtli* and describes them as having a long hairy coat that becomes shaggy with age; small, narrow ears; a round, broad face, almost like the face of a man; and a thick snout. They were known to be strong and brave, like a warrior.[354]

Nonordinary Realm Associations: Middleworld and Underworld
Spiritual and Shapeshifting Medicine: strength, courage, unrestraint, and independence
Symbolism Meanings

◄ Stand tall, and be confident and self-assured, especially in the face of any adversity.

◄ Be impeccable with your words, and refrain from using them to lash out. Take a step back, be firm and honest and at the same time compassionate.

◄ Give yourself time to rest, rejuvenate, and reflect in solitude.

◄ Use your healing gifts to help others.

❀ Wolf ❀

Wolves are independent and very territorial, yet can work incredibly well with their community or pack of wolves to hunt and find shelter. Most wolves are nocturnal and travel in packs, which often consist of their nuclear family—their mate and offspring. They may travel alone temporarily, until they find their mate to create a pack or team up with another pack of wolves. Typically, they are monogamous, but if one of the pair dies, the other usually finds another partner. Their howls are quite loud and can be heard up to about fifty miles away. They howl to request their pack to join them in a hunt, warn their pack of danger, locate one another, and communicate between long distances. They were known by Central Mexicans to be strong and courageous animals, and their breath was believed to be supernatural and potentially poisonous.[355] Tezcatlipoca was known for being able to shapeshift into a wolf and warn people on the road that danger was up ahead.[356]

Nonordinary Realm Associations: Middleworld and Underworld

Spiritual and Shapeshifting Medicine: bravery, intuition, power, and discernment

Symbolism Meanings

◄ Be discerning as to whom you give your loyalty and trust to. Make sure they demonstrate that they are worthy of it.

◄ Consider taking a trip on your own even if just for the day. During this time, reflect on what you identify in your life as being either flexible or nonnegotiable.

◄ Value the people in your life that have demonstrated their loyalty to you, and do something to show your gratitude for them.

◄ There is someone in your life whose actions you need to objectively evaluate and whom you may need to consider stepping away from.

☀ Woodpecker ☀

Woodpeckers are generally diurnal, solitary, arboreal birds of wooded habitats. They have strong bills for drilling and drumming on trees, which they do largely for courtship, to mark their territory, and, of course, to obtain access to food, insects, and larvae with their long sticky tongues. Because of this distinctive communicative drumming, they tended to have strong augural associations. In Maya art, they appeared in starry contexts on imagery of sky bands.[357] In the Books of Chilam Balam of Kaua and Mani, the Maya identify the woodpecker as helping humankind to obtain maize by pecking the rock under which it was hidden to find the weakest point.[358] The Central Mexicans would say that if a woodpecker was shrieking, it was angry and this was a bad omen. However, if it was whistling, it was happy, and it was believed that great fortune would come to the listener(s).[359]

Nonordinary Realm Associations: Upperworld
Spiritual and Shapeshifting Medicine: persistence, independence, calculation, and perception
Symbolism Meanings

◄ Remember that healing and developing self-understanding is a process of peeling away layers. You may have worked on the same issue on another occasion, but now you are ultimately approaching it—or possibly another aspect of it—as a different person. Be patient, understanding, loving, and tender with yourself.

◄ Listen for and understand the intent behind what is being said rather than simply hearing the words.

◄ Dig deeper into whatever you are questioning, and let your intuition guide you to the truth.

◄ Tune in to your personal rhythms and the time(s) you are most productive. Honor yourself, and work toward planning your activities accordingly.

✸ Wood Stork ✸

Wood storks are large wading birds that are about three and a half feet tall with a wingspan of at least five feet. Their plumage is primarily white with the exception of the tail that is black with a purple-green sheen, and their heads and necks are featherless and dark gray. They can usually be found in freshwater habitats, and they nest colonially, with about twenty-five nests in a tree. These birds have a large appetite and eat more than a pound of food a day. They obtain their food through a "grope feeding" method. They submerge their massive beaks in the water while groping for food. As soon as they feel their food, they immediately toss their heads back and swallow. When flying, they alternate between flapping and gliding. The Central Mexicans respected this bird and left it alone. They considered it be an evil omen. If it was caught, they believed that the worst would come—lords would die, and if war broke out, warriors would lose their lives in battle.[360]

Nonordinary Realm Associations: Middleworld and Underworld

Spiritual and Shapeshifting Medicine: prodigiousness, prohibition, domestication, and determination

Symbolism Meanings

◄ Be patient and persistent in what you are looking for; do not give up. You will find that diamond in the rough.

◄ In light of virtual online ways of communicating and connecting, expand your understanding of community, and let your support network grow.

◄ Do not hesitate to release something that does not serve you or feels toxic to you in any way.

◄ Make sure you do not burn yourself out, and provide time for yourself to rest and revitalize.

Notes

Introduction to Ancient Mesoamerican and Curanderismo Animal Symbolism

1. Ruiz de Alarcón, *Aztec Sorcerers,* 131, 148, 150, 152, 154, 156, 161, 164.
2. De la Garza, *Sueno y Extasis,* 60; Boone, *Cycles of Time and Meaning,* 27.
3. Velásquez García, "Nuevas ideas," 573.
4. Mazariegos, *Art and Myth,* 28–29.
5. Bell, *Ritual,* 267.
6. López Austin, *Myths of the Opossum,* 14.
7. Mazariegos, *Art and Myth,* 23.
8. López Austin, *Myths of the Opossum,* 247–59; Mazariegos, "Of Birds and Insects," 45, 58; Mazariegos, *Art and Myth,* 27.
9. Benson, *Birds and Beasts,* 8–9, 21, 52.
10. Benson, 12–13.
11. Ortiz de Montellano, *Aztec Medicine,* 172, 177.
12. Ortiz de Montellano, 179, 180.
13. Ortiz de Montellano, *Aztec Medicine,* 133, 177; De la Serna, *Tratado De Las Idolatrías,* 81.
14. Peterson and Green, *Precolumbian Flora and Fauna,* 12.
15. Benson, *Birds and Beasts,* 12.
16. López Austin, *Cuerpo humano,* 1:226, 251.

1. Animal Contact and Medicine in the Nonordinary Realms

1. Benson, *Birds and Beasts,* 12.
2. Buenaflor, *Curanderismo Soul Retrieval,* 41.
3. Aguilar-Moreno, *Handbook to Life,* 302–3; Foster, *Handbook to Life,* 28.
4. Harner, *Way of the Shaman,* 52.
5. Buenaflor, *Curanderismo Soul Retrieval,* 43–45.

6. Foster, *Handbook to Life*, 161, 298.

7. León-Portilla, *Aztec Thought*, 31.

8. León-Portilla, *Aztec Thought*, 50

9. Aguilar-Moreno, *Handbook to Life*, 138.

10. León-Portilla, *Aztec Thought*, 51-52; Aguilar-Moreno, *Handbook to Life*, 303.

11. Milbrath, *Star Gods*, 70; Craine and Reindorp, *Codex Perez*, 49-50; Roys, *Book of Chilam Balam*, 110-111.

12. León-Portilla, *Aztec Thought*, 126; Sahagún, *Florentine Codex*, 3:49, 6:13, 162.

13. Peterson and Green, *Precolumbian Flora and Fauna*, 20–21.

14. De Landa, *Yucatán Before and After*, 57–58.

15. Taube, "Flower Mountain," 80.

16. Taube, "Flower Mountain," 80–82; Taube, "At Dawn's Edge," 147.

17. Peterson and Green, *Precolumbian Flora and Fauna*, 34.

18. De la Serna, *Tratado De Las Idolatrías*, 184; Pineda, "La fauna de Ehécatl," 259.

19. De la Serna, *Tratado De Las Idolatrías*, 184, 201.

20. Benson, *Birds and Beasts*, 79.

21. Benson, 73.

22. Peterson and Green, *Precolumbian Flora and Fauna*, 20–21.

23. Freidel, Schele, and Parker, *Maya Cosmos*, 82–84, 92; Milbrath, *Star Gods of the Maya*, 253; Foster, *Handbook to Life*, 161.

24. Freidel, Schele, and Parker, *Maya Cosmos*, 426n64; Schlesinger, *Animals and Plants of the Ancient Maya*, 66, 160.

25. Foster, *Handbook to Life*, 180–82.

26. Burkhart, "Flowery Heaven," 99; Taube, "Flower Mountain," 80.

27. Ortiz de Montellano, *Aztec Medicine*, 43, citing Carrasco, *Quetzalcoatl*, 71; Aguilar-Moreno, *Handbook to Life*, 228.

28. Aguilar-Moreno, *Handbook to Life*, 220; Durán, *Book of Gods*, 78.

29. Benson, *Birds and Beasts*, 43; Peterson and Green, *Precolumbian Flora and Fauna*, 22; Taylor, "Painted Ladies," 519; Schele and Miller, *Blood of Kings*, 46.

30. Benson, *Birds and Beasts*, 52; Peterson and Green, *Precolumbian Flora and Fauna*, 56.

31. Peterson and Green, *Precolumbian Flora and Fauna*, 46; Milbrath, *Star Gods of the Maya*, 119; Stuart, *Order of Days*, 90; Foster, *Handbook to Life*, 161; Brady and Ashmore, "Mountains, Caves, Water," 127.

32. Scherer, *Mortuary Landscapes*, 63, 107.

33. Foster, *Handbook to Life*, 182; Bernatz, "Redefining God L," 163.

34. Schlesinger, *Animals and Plants of the Ancient Maya*, 183; Foster, *Handbook to Life*, 311; Sahagún, *Florentine Codex*, 11:16.

35. Peterson and Green, *Precolumbian Flora and Fauna,* 8.

36. Sahagún, *Florentine Codex,* 11:61; Schlesinger, *Animals and Plants of the Ancient Maya,* 226.

37. Thompson, *Maya Hieroglyphic Writing,* 124; De Landa, *Yucatán Before and After,* 65–66.

38. León-Portilla, *Aztec Thought,* 124; Aguilar-Moreno, *Handbook to Life,* 139, 165; Sahagún, *Florentine Codex,* 3:41.

39. Taube, *Legendary Past,* 37–39; Boone, *Cycles of Time and Meaning,* 192, 204; León-Portilla, *Aztec Thought,* 108–10.

40. Taube, "Ancient and Contemporary Maya Conceptions," 466; Stuart, *Order of Days,* 90; Foster, *Handbook to Life,* 161; Brady and Ashmore, "Mountains, Caves, Water," 127.

41. León-Portilla et al., *Language of Kings,* 426–33; Scherer, *Mortuary Landscapes,* 47.

42. Benson, *Birds and Beasts,* 68; Pineda, "La fauna de Ehécatl," 291.

43. Benson, *Birds and Beasts,* 117; Quenon and Le Fort, "Rebirth and Resurrection," 886.

44. Sahagún, *Florentine Codex,* 11:1–3; Peterson and Green, *Precolumbian Flora and Fauna*, 90; Fernández, *Dioses prehispánicos de México,* 142.

45. Peterson and Green, *Precolumbian Flora and Fauna,* 56.

46. Bernatz, "Redefining God L," 163.

47. Carrasco, "Portals, Turtles, and Mythic Places," 395; Stuart, *Inscriptions,* 70–73.

2. Diverse Shapeshifting Practices and Their Many Benefits

1. Gossen, "Animal Souls," 81.

2. Furst, *Natural History,* 171; Álvarez Esteban, "La entidada animica," 5.

3. López Austin, *Cuerpo humano,* 1:431; López Austin, *Tamoanchan,* 138.

4. Maffie, *Aztec Philosophy,* 45, 271; citing López Austin, *Human Body,* 1:348; Furst, *Natural History,* 126, 180–83; León-Portilla, *Aztec Thought,* 114; Aguilar-Moreno, *Handbook to Life,* 172; Ortiz de Montellano, *Aztec Medicine,* 45.

5. Sahagún, *Florentine Codex,* 6:202, 205–206.

6. López Austin, *Human Body,* 1:226, 251.

7. López Austin, "Cuarenta clases," 98–99; *Cuerpo humano,* 1:424.

8. Aguilar-Moreno, *Handbook to Life,* 90.

9. Sahagún, *Florentine Codex,* 4 and 5:42, 101; Aguilar-Moreno, *Handbook to Life,* 90.

10. Roys, *Ritual of the Bacabs,* 168–170.

11. López Austin, *Cuerpo humano,* 1:419.

12. López Austin, 1:427–28.

13. Zender, "On the Morphology of Intimate Possession," 202n131, 203.

14. Houston and Stuart, "Way Glyph," 454–55; Velásquez García, "Nuevas ideas," 567; Gossen, "Animal Souls," 98.

15. Houston and Stuart, "Way Glyph," 462; Stuart, "Way Beings," 1.

16. Grube and Nahm. "Census of Xibalba," 694; Scherer, *Mortuary Landscapes,* 46; Foster, *Handbook to Life,* 179.

17. Fridberg, "Peccaries in Ancient Maya," 24.

18. López Austin, *Cuerpo humano,* 1:217, 252; Sahagún, *Florentine Codex,* 10:130–31.

19. Maffie, *Aztec Philosophy,* 506; León-Portilla, *Aztec Thought,* 50.

20. Christenson, *Popol Vuh,* 57n44.

21. Aguilar-Moreno, *Handbook to Life,* 172.

22. Ortiz de Montellano, *Aztec Medicine,* 61; López-Austin, *Cuerpo humano,* 1:231–32.

23. Burkhart, *Slippery Earth,* 61–62, 92, 171–77.

24. Aguilar-Moreno, *Handbook to Life,* 172.

25. Sahagún, *Florentine Codex,* 2:120–21

26. Sahagún, 2:156–57.

27. Durán, *Book of Gods,* 244.

28. Maffie, *Aztec Philosophy,* 45, 271; citing López Austin, *Human Body,* 1:348; Furst, *Natural History,* 126.

29. Scherer, *Mortuary Landscapes,* 56–58; Taube, "At Dawn's Edge," 147; Freidel, Schele, and Parker, *Maya Cosmos,* 245.

30. Scherer, *Mortuary Landscapes,* 60, 73, 121.

31. Foster, *Handbook to Life,* 193.

32. Maffie, *Aztec Philosophy,* 214.

33. Maffie, 271, 424.

34. Maffie, *Aztec Philosophy,* 180; Ortiz de Montellano, *Aztec Medicine,* 134.

35. Ortiz de Montellano, *Aztec Medicine,* 33, 222.

36. Ortiz de Montellano, 152–54, 171.

37. Ortiz de Montellano, *Aztec Medicine,* 153; Maffie, *Aztec Philosophy,* 60–61.

38. Ruiz de Alarcón, *Aztec Sorcerers,* 223–29.

39. Sahagún, *Florentine Codex,* 4–5:101–02; Furst, *Natural History,* 180–83; Ortiz de Montellano, *Aztec Medicine,* 45; López Austin, *Cuerpo humano,* 1:378.

40. López Austin, *Cuerpo humano,* 1:430–31.

41. Aguilar-Moreno, *Handbook to Life,* 172; López Austin, *Cuerpo humano,* 1:184, 194, 257–58.

42. Furst, *Natural History,* 154–55; citing Molina, *Vocabulario,* 36r., 36v.

43. López Austin, *Cuerpo humano,* 1:260–61.

44. Aguilar-Moreno, *Handbook to Life,* 172; Furst, *Natural History,* 143.

45. Sahagún, *Florentine Codex,* 6:44.

46. Furst, *Natural History,* 168–69.

47. López Austin, *Cuerpo humano,* 1:430–31.

48. Taube, "Flower Mountain," 70–71.

49. Houston, Stuart, and Taube, *Memory of Bones,* 270; Taube, "Symbolism of Jade," 74.

50. Houston, Stuart, and Taube, *Memory of Bones,* 276.

51. Moreno, "Los espiritus del sueno," 11.

52. Stone, *Images from the Underworld,* 39; Taube, "Ancient and Contemporary Maya Conceptions," 481.

53. Velásquez García, "Nuevas ideas," 573.

54. Velásquez García, "Nuevas ideas," 561; Foster, *Handbook to Life,* 155

55. De la Serna, *Tratado De Las Idolatrías,* 52.

56. Ruiz de Alarcón, *Aztec Sorcerers,* 64.

57. Ruiz de Alarcón, *Aztec Sorcerers,* 64; De la Serna, *Tratado De Las Idolatrías,* 62.

58. Ruiz de Alarcón, 65; De la Serna, 63.

59. Ruiz de Alarcón, *Aztec Sorcerers,* 65.

Part 2. Animal Allies A to Z

1. Sahagún, *Florentine Codex,* 11:33.

2. De Landa, *Yucatán Before and After,* 100.

3. Schlesinger, *Animals and Plants of the Ancient Maya,* 240.

4. Milbrath, *Star Gods of the Maya,* 111; Cogolludo, *Historia de Yucatán,* 218–19.

5. Taube, *Legendary Past,* 39.

6. Torres, "Estudios de cultura Náhuatl," 387.

7. De la Serna, *Tratado De Las Idolatrías,* 188.

8. Peterson and Green, *Precolumbian Flora and Fauna,* 56.

9. Benson, *Birds and Beasts,* 58–59.

10. De Landa, *Yucatán Before and After,* 110.

11. Sahagún, *Florentine Codex,* 11:28.

12. Nequatewa, Edmund, *Truth of a Hopi,* 10–17; Tedlock, *Popol Vuh* (1996), 297n152.

13. Peterson and Green, *Precolumbian Flora and Fauna,* 91, 108.

14. Schlesinger, *Animals and Plants of the Ancient Maya,* 167; Seler, Thompson, and Comparato, *Collected Works,* 176.

15. Benson, *Birds and Beasts*, 53–54.

16. Christenson, *Popol Vuh*, 160–64.

17. Thompson, *Maya Hieroglyphic Writing*, 73–74.

18. Milbrath, "Seasonal Imagery," 124.

19. Fernández, *Dioses prehispánicos de México*, 142.

20. Boone, *Cycles of Time and Meaning*, 204.

21. Zrałka, Helmke, Sotelo, and Koszkul, "Discovery of a Beehive," 525; De la Serna, *Tratado De Las Idolatrías*, 129.

22. Christenson, *Popol Vuh*, 183n469.

23. Benson, *Birds and Beasts*, 33.

24. Grube and Nahm, "A Sign for the Syllable mi," 22.

25. De Landa, *Yucatán Before and After*, 73, 76.

26. Roys, *Chilam Balam of Chumayel*, 2.

27. Milbrath, "Seasonal Imagery," 124.

28. De la Serna, *Tratado De Las Idolatrías*, 125, 127.

29. López Austin, *Myths of the Opossum*, 112; Ruiz de Alarcón, *Aztec Sorcerers*, 76.

30. Sahagún, *Florentine Codex*, 11:31.

31. Taube, "At Dawn's Edge," 147, 170, 182.

32. Durán, *Book of Gods*, 188, 414.

33. León-Portilla, *Aztec Thought*, 126; Sahagún, *Florentine Codex*, 3:49, 6:13, 162.

34. Milbrath, "Xochiquetzal," 40, fig. 8, 41.

35. Milbrath, "Seasonal Imagery," 124.

36. Taube, "At Dawn's Edge," 182.

37. Velásquez García, "Reflections on the Codex Style," 6; Taube, "Temple of Quetzalcoatl," 59–68, Taube, "Turquoise Hearth," 285.

38. Blainey, "Techniques of Luminosity," 182.

39. Scherer, *Mortuary Landscapes*, 63, 107.

40. Taube, *Major Gods of Ancient Yucatán*, 38.

41. Foster, *Handbook to Life*, 91.

42. Velásquez García, "Maya Flood Myth," 7; Bernatz, "Redefining God L," 163.

43. Bernatz, "Redefining God L," 163.

44. Foster, *Handbook to Life*, 182.

45. Velásquez García, "Nuevas ideas," 422, 424.

46. López Austin, *Myths of the Opossum*, 51; Taube, *Legendary Past*, 70, 73.

47. Taube, *Major Gods of Ancient Yucatán*, 40.

48. Boone, *Cycles of Time and Meaning*, 197.

49. Durán, *Book of Gods*, 399.

50. De la Serna, *Tratado De Las Idolatrías,* 83.
51. Milbrath, "Seasonal Imagery," 119.
52. Kettunen, "Nasal Motifs," 747.
53. Taube, "Flower Mountain," 76.
54. Quenon and Le Fort, "Rebirth and Resurrection," 891; Christenson, *Popol Vuh,* 149.
55. Grofe, *Recipe for Rebirth,* 42.
56. Taube, *Legendary Past,* 35–36.
57. Turner, "Cultures at the Crossroads," 55.
58. Taube, "Maws of Heaven and Hell," 406.
59. Taube, "Maws of Heaven and Hell," 410–13; Velásquez García, "Reflections on the Codex Style," 10.
60. Seler, Thompson, and Comparato, *Collected Works,* 334.
61. Taube, "Maws of Heaven and Hell," 410–13; Scherer, *Mortuary Landscapes,* 132.
62. Zender, "Study of Classic Maya Priesthood," 69; Martin, Berrin, and Miller, *Courtly Art,* 57.
63. Mazariegos, *Art and Myth,* 123; Houston and Stuart, "Way Glyph," 456.
64. Taube, "Maws of Heaven and Hell," 406.
65. Durán, *Book of Gods,* 115–17.
66. Peterson and Green, *Precolumbian Flora and Fauna,* 56.
67. Benson, *Birds and Beasts,* 52, 56.
68. Christenson, *Popol Vuh,* 62.
69. Grofe, *Recipe for Rebirth,* 41–42.
70. Christenson, *Popol Vuh,* 181n458.
71. Christenson, 50–53, 53n16.
72. Sahagún, *Florentine Codex,* 11:7.
73. Ortiz de Montellano, *Aztec Medicine,* 69; López Austin, *Cuerpo humano,* 1:422.
74. Sahagún, *Florentine Codex,* vols. 4 and 5:101.
75. Aguilar-Moreno, *Handbook to Life,* 202–03.
76. Seler, Thompson, and Comparato, *Collected Works,* 194.
77. Boone, *Cycles of Time and Meaning,* 104–106.
78. Thompson, *Maya History and Religion,* 353.
79. Hernández and Bricker, "Inauguration of Planting," 291.
80. Sahagún, *Florentine Codex,* 11:51.
81. Peterson and Green, *Precolumbian Flora and Fauna,* 22; Boone, *Cycles of Time and Meaning,* 186; Benson, *Birds and* Beasts, 35.
82. Peterson and Green, *Precolumbian Flora and Fauna,* 22.

83. Sahagún, *Florentine Codex,* 11:15.

84. Velásquez García, "Maya Flood Myth," 5–8.

85. Carrasco, "Portals, Turtles, and Mythic Places," 395–96; Stuart, *Inscriptions,* 70–73.

86. Taube, *Legendary Past,* 55.

87. Milbrath, *Star Gods of the Maya,* 76.

88. Taylor, "Painted Ladies," 523.

89. Mazariegos, *Art and Myth,* 233–34, 237.

90. Boone, *Cycles of Time and Meaning,* 186; Milbrath, *Star Gods of the Maya,* 74.

91. Durán, *Book of Gods,* 399, 400–1.

92. Sahagún, *Florentine Codex,* vols. 4 and 5:9–10.

93. Sahagún, 11:16.

94. Peterson and Green, *Precolumbian Flora and Fauna,* 8; Schlesinger, *Animals and Plants of the Ancient Maya,* 161; López-Austin, *Myths of the Opossum,* 17; Benson, *Birds and Beasts,* 23.

95. Foster, *Handbook to Life,* 311, 335.

96. Mazariegos, *Art and Myth,* 63; Taube, *Legendary Past,* 36.

97. Sahagún, *Florentine Codex,* 11:16.

98. Seler, Thompson, and Comparato, *Collected Works,* 179.

99. Ortiz de Montellano, *Aztec Medicine,* 49; Sahagún, *Florentine Codex,* 3:44.

100. Durán, *Book of Gods,* 401.

101. López Austin, *Cuerpo humano,* 1:419; Sahagún, *Florentine Codex,* vols. 4 and 5:42.

102. Peterson and Green, *Precolumbian Flora and Fauna,* 68.

103. Taube, *Legendary Past,* 16–17.

104. Boone, *Cycles of Time and Meaning,* 192, 204; León-Portilla, *Aztec Thought,* 108–110.

105. Maffie, *Aztec Philosophy,* 207.

106. Milbrath, "Seasonal Imagery," 130.

107. Kettunen, "Nasal Motifs," 99n65; Hernández, "Llego el caiman," 194–95.

108. Hernández, "Llego el caiman," 217, 220.

109. De la Garza, *Sueno y Extasis,* 150.

110. Taube, "Flower Mountain," 80.

111. Taube, "Symbolism of Jade," 39.

112. Ingalls, "Quadripartite Badge," 11; Velásquez García, "Maya Flood Myth," 2–4.

113. Thompson, *Maya Hieroglyphic Writing,* 87.

114. Ortiz de Montellano, *Aztec Medicine,* 178; Sahagún, *Florentine Codex,* 11:48.

115. Mazariegos, "Of Birds and Insects," 46.

116. López Austin, *Tamoanchan, Tlalocan,* 226–27.

117. León-Portilla, *Aztec Thought,* 125.

118. Benson, *Birds and Beasts,* 31.

119. Turner, "Cultures at the Crossroads," 94–95; Taube, *Olmec Art,* 169–73; Taube, Saturno, Stuart, and Hurst, "Murals of San Bartolo," 49.

120. Aguilar-Moreno, *Handbook to Life,* 148–50.

121. Peterson and Green, *Precolumbian Flora and Fauna,* 76.

122. Aguilar-Moreno, *Handbook to Life,* 178; Peterson and Green, *Precolumbian Flora and Fauna,* 10; Taube, "Turquoise Hearth," 321.

123. Velásquez García, "Nuevas ideas," 561.

124. Taube, "Symbolism of Jade," 43.

125. Peterson and Green, *Precolumbian Flora and Fauna,* 18.

126. Durán, *Book of Gods,* 187.

127. Sahagún, *Florentine Codex,* 11:40.

128. Taube, *Legendary Past,* 42.

129. Durán, *Book of Gods,* 402.

130. Ortiz de Montellano, *Aztec Medicine,* 178; Sahagún, *Florentine Codex,* 11:92.

131. Christenson, *Popol Vuh,* 145n367; Sahagún, *Florentine Codex,* 11:43.

132. Benson, *Birds and Beasts,* 82; Christenson, *Popol Vuh,* 145.

133. Christenson, *Popol Vuh,* 145n367.

134. Christenson, *Popol Vuh,* 145n367; Roys, *Ritual of the Bacabs,* 17; Sahagún, *Florentine Codex,* 2:16–18, 3:251.

135. Roys, *Ritual of the Bacabs,* 17.

136. Sahagún, *Florentine Codex,* 2:16–18, 3:251.

137. López Austin, *Myths of the Opossum,* 161.

138. Aguilar-Moreno, *Handbook to Life,* 295; Durán, *Book of Gods,* 243; Taube, "At Dawn's Edge," 148.

139. Sahagún, *Florentine Codex,* 7:163.

140. Peterson and Green, *Precolumbian Flora and Fauna,* 34.

141. Houston, *Hieroglyphs and History at Dos Pilas,* 101.

142. Lopes, *Some Notes on Fireflies,* 6.

143. Milbrath, *Star Gods of the Maya,* 249, 251, 253.

144. Christenson, *Popol Vuh,* 153.

145. Christenson, 181n458.

146. Roys, *Chilam Balam of Chumayel,* 9.

147. Christenson, *Popol Vuh,* 137–38.

148. Peterson and Green, *Precolumbian Flora and Fauna,* 46.

149. Ashmore, "Site-Planning Principles," 205.

150. Milbrath, *Star Gods of the Maya,* 119.

151. Proskouriakoff, "Portraits of Women in Maya Art," 348; Milbrath, *Star Gods of the Maya.*

152. Carrasco, "Mask Flange," 149, 202.

153. De la Serna, *Tratado De Las Idolatrías,* 188.

154. Roys, *Ritual of the Bacabs,* Ritual 63.

155. Roys, 91n67.

156. Peterson and Green, *Precolumbian Flora and Fauna,* 56.

157. Grube and Nahm, "Census of Xibalba," 704.

158. Burdick, "Text and Image," 189.

159. Hull, Wright, and Fergus, "Avian Actors," 353.

160. Milbrath, "Seasonal Imagery," 131.

161. Taube, *Legendary Past,* 42.

162. Stuart and Stuart, *Palenque,* 226–28.

163. Milbrath, *Star Gods of the Maya,* 151.

164. Looper, "Women-Men," 178–79.

165. Durán, *Book of Gods,* 99, 105.

166. Mexicolore, "God of the Month," 1.

167. Seler, Thompson, and Comparato, *Collected Works,* 269.

168. Peterson and Green, *Precolumbian Flora and Fauna,* 8, 20–21; Milbrath, *Star Gods of the Maya,* 94; Benson, *Birds and Beasts,* 77–78.

169. Benson, *Birds and Beasts,* 77.

170. Peterson and green, *Precolumbian Flora and Fauna,* 20–21.

171. Sahagún, *Florentine Codex,* 11:24; Durán, *Book of Gods,* 72–73.

172. Sahagún, *Florentine Codex,* 3:49; León-Portilla, *Aztec Thought,* 126.

173. López Austin, *Cuerpo humano,* 1:422–23.

174. Milbrath, "Seasonal Imagery," 124.

175. Mazariegos, *Art and Myth,* 93–94.

176. Mazariegos, 87.

177. Hull, Wright, and Fergus, "Avian Actors," 359; Stone and Zender, *Reading Maya Art,* 209.

178. Durán, *Book of Gods,* 400.

179. Sahagún, *Florentine Codex,* 11:61.

180. Benson, *Birds and Beasts,* 102.

181. Schlesinger, *Animals and Plants of the Ancient Maya,* 226.

182. Kettunen, "Nasal Motifs," 5.

183. Peterson and Green, *Precolumbian Flora and Fauna,* 90.

184. Benson, *Birds and Beasts,* 46.

185. Foster, *Handbook to Life,* 166.

186. Taube, *Major Gods,* 54.

187. Stuart and Stuart, *Palenque,* 190.

188. Stuart and Stuart, 194, 209.

189. Taube, *Major Gods of Ancient Yucatán,* 101.

190. Benson, *Birds and Beasts,* 46.

191. Taube, *Major Gods of Ancient Yucatán,* 54; Milbrath, *Star Gods of the Maya,* 105–6; Taube, "Birth Vase," 667.

192. Durán, *Book of Gods,* 187.

193. Taube, *Legendary Past,* 42.

194. Sahagún, *Florentine Codex,* vols. 4 and 5:33–35.

195. Benson, *Birds and Beasts,* 46; Olivier, *Mockeries and Metamorphoses,* 38.

196. Durán, *Book of Gods,* 402.

197. Furst, *Natural History,* 182.

198. Christenson, *Popol Vuh,* 52.

199. Christenson, 67–69.

200. Taube, *Olmec Art,* 104.

201. Benson, *Birds and Beasts,* 75.

202. Turner, "Cultures at the Crossroads," 75.

203. Milbrath, *Star Gods of the Maya,* 94.

204. Mazariegos, *Art and Myth,* 131.

205. Milbrath, *Star Gods of the Maya,* 58; Seler, Thompson, and Comparato, *Collected Works,* 225.

206. Benson, *Birds and Beasts,* 60; Foster, *Handbook to Life,* 91.

207. Benson, *Birds and Beasts,* 52.

208. Benson, 60.

209. Peterson and Green, *Precolumbian Flora and Fauna,* 58.

210. Milbrath, *Star Gods of the Maya,* 219; Tedlock, *Popol Vuh* (1985), 342.

211. Milbrath, *Star Gods of the Maya,* 225.

212. Taube, *Legendary Past,* 34–35.

213. Durán, *Book of Gods,* 401.

214. Seler, Thompson, and Comparato, *Collected Works,* 167.

215. Sahagún, *Florentine Codex,* 11:17.

216. De la Serna, *Tratado De Las Idolatrías,* 188.

217. Seler, Thompson, and Comparato, *Collected Works,* 263.

218. Sahagún, *Florentine Codex,* 11:25.

219. López Austin, *Myths of the Opossum,* 53.

220. Sahagún, *Florentine Codex,* 11:1–3.

221. López Austin, *Myths of the Opossum*, 4; Benson, *Birds and Beasts*, 66.

222. López Austin, *Myths of the Opossum*, 3.

223. López Austin, 56.

224. López Austin, 167.

225. Taube, "Ancient and Contemporary Maya Conceptions," 483.

226. López Austin, *Myths of the Opossum*, 56.

227. López Austin, *Myths of the Opossum*, 5; Seler, Thompson, and Comparato, *Collected Works*, 197, 200.

228. Sahagún, *Florentine Codex*, 11:12; Seler, Thompson, and Comparato, *Collected Works*, 200.

229. Seler, Thompson, and Comparato, *Collected Works*, 253; Benson, *Birds and Beasts*, 87; Sahagún, *Florentine Codex*, 11:42.

230. Peterson and Green, *Precolumbian Flora and Fauna*, 90.

231. Schlesinger, *Animals and Plants of the Ancient Maya*, 216.

232. Taube, *Legendary Past*, 57.

233. Schlesinger, *Animals and Plants of the Ancient Maya*, 217.

234. Taube, *Legendary Past*, 80–81; Foster, *Handbook to Life*, 168–69.

235. Ortiz de Montellano, *Aztec Medicine*, 140.

236. Aguilar-Moreno, *Handbook to Life*, 160; De la Serna, *Tratado De Las Idolatrías*, 196; Peterson and Green, *Precolumbian Flora and Fauna*, 90.

237. Sahagún, *Primeros Memoriales*, 174.

238. Fridberg, "Peccaries in Ancient Maya," 29, 60.

239. Milbrath, *Star Gods of the Maya*, 76.

240. Peterson and Green, *Precolumbian Flora and Fauna*, 91.

241. Fridberg, "Peccaries in Ancient Maya," 24–25.

242. Grube and Nahm. "A Census of Xibalba," 698, figs. 3.1, 3.2, and 3.3.

243. Fridberg, "Peccaries in Ancient Maya," 24–25.

244. Pineda, "La fauna de Ehécatl," 282.

245. Sahagún, *Florentine Codex*, 11:29–30.

246. Seler, Thompson, and Comparato, *Collected Works*, 200, 203.

247. Seler, Thompson, and Comparato, 176.

248. Thompson, *Maya History and Religion*, 312, 328.

249. Burdick, "Text and Image," 158.

250. Saturno, Rossi, Stuart, and Hurst, "A Maya Curia Regis," 10.

251. Sahagún, *Florentine Codex*, 11:32.

252. Sahagún, 32–33, 244.

253. Aguilera, "El Simbolismo del quetzal," 222.

254. Benson, *Birds and Beasts*, 75–76; Taube, *Major Gods of Ancient Yucatán*, 83.

255. Furst, *Natural History,* 182.

256. Aguilera, "El Simbolismo del quetzal," 230.

257. Seler, Thompson, and Comparato, *Collected Works,* 225.

258. Peterson and Green, *Precolumbian Flora and Fauna,* 22.

259. Bernatz, "Redefining God L," 167; Martin, Berrin, and Miller, *Courtly Art,* 61.

260. Taylor, "Painted Ladies," 174.

261. Benson, *Birds and Beasts,* 42.

262. Sahagún, *Florentine Codex,* 3:1, 7:4–8; Ruiz de Alarcón, *Aztec Sorcerers,* 31, 100, 101.

263. Boone, *Cycles of Time and Meaning,* 186.

264. Thompson, *Maya Hieroglyphic Writing,* 11–12, 84, 133.

265. Benson, *Birds and Beasts,* 43.

266. Sahagún, *Florentine Codex,* 11:9.

267. Seler, Thompson, and Comparato, *Collected Works,* 200.

268. Scherer, *Mortuary Landscapes,* 16, 246n99.

269. Christenson, *Popol Vuh,* 140–143.

270. Sahagún, *Florentine Codex,* 11:6.

271. Saturno, Rossi, Stuart, and Hurst, "A Maya Curia Regis," 4.

272. Roys, *Ritual of the Bacabs,* 31, 134.

273. Milbrath, *Star Gods of the Maya,* 266.

274. Durán, *Book of Gods,* 115–17.

275. De la Serna, *Tratado De Las Idolatría*s, 226–29; Ruiz de Alarcón, *Aztec Sorcerers,* 293, 295.

276. Freidel, Schele, and Parker, *Maya Cosmos,* 207; Aguilar-Moreno, *Handbook to Life,* 213–14.

277. De la Garza, *Sueno y Extasis,* 152.

278. Benson, *Birds and Beasts,* 106; Peterson and Green, *Precolumbian Flora and Fauna,* 36.

279. Taube, *Major Gods of Ancient Yucatán,* 17, 19, 22.

280. Taube, 101.

281. Foster, *Handbook to Life,* 182.

282. Mazariegos, *Art and Myth,* 122.

283. Foster, *Handbook to Life,* 188.

284. Taube, *Major Gods of Ancient Yucatán,* 15, fig. h.

285. Taube, *Major Gods of Ancient Yucatán,* 22; Aguilar-Moreno, *Handbook to Life,* 178.

286. Mazariegos, *Art and Myth,* 118.

287. Boone, *Cycles of Time and Meaning,* 52.

288. Durán, *Book of Gods,* 400.

289. Ruiz de Alarcón, *Aztec Sorcerers,* 34, 97, 98.

290. Furst, *Natural History,* 106.

291. Sahagún, *Florentine Codex,* 11:76.

292. Milbrath, *Star Gods of the Maya,* 250, 253, 258.

293. Ortiz de Montellano, *Aztec Medicine,* 69; López Austin, *Cuerpo humano,* 1:194, 422.

294. De la Garza, *Sueno y Extasis,* 99.

295. Sahagún, *Florentine Codex,* 175; De la Serna, *Tratado De Las Idolatrías,* 187.

296. Scherer, *Mortuary Landscapes,* 70.

297. Scherer, 137.

298. Taylor, "Painted Ladies," 177–79.

299. Peterson and Green, *Precolumbian Flora and Fauna,* 78.

300. Quenon and Le Fort, "Rebirth and Resurrection," 889.

301. Peterson and Green, *Precolumbian Flora and Fauna,* 78.

302. Benson, *Birds and Beasts,* 125; Aguilar-Moreno, *Handbook to Life,* 178; Pineda, "La fauna de Ehécatl," 270.

303. Seler, Thompson, and Comparato, *Collected Works,* 339.

304. Benson, *Birds and Beasts,* 124.

305. Peterson and Green, *Precolumbian Flora and Fauna,* 78.

306. Taylor, "Painted Ladies," 178.

307. Benson, *Birds and Beasts,* 129.

308. Scherer, *Mortuary Landscapes,* 116, 169.

309. Seler, Thompson, and Comparato, *Collected Works,* 247.

310. Benson, *Birds and Beasts,* 66.

311. Ashmore, "Gender and Landscapes," 211.

312. Taube, *Major Gods of Ancient Yucatán,* 95, fig. c.

313. Taube, 95, fig. b.

314. Freidel, Schele, and Parker, *Maya Cosmos,* 126.

315. Roys, *Ritual of the Bacabs,* 53.

316. Boone, *Cycles of Time and Meaning,* 186.

317. Milbrath, "Gender Roles," 66–67.

318. De la Serna, *Tratado De Las Idolatrías,* 200.

319. Sahagún, *Florentine Codex,* 11:10.

320. Seler, Thompson, and Comparato, *Collected Works,* 206.

321. Houston, Stuart, and Taube, "Image and Text," 513.

322. Benson, *Birds and Beasts,* 118.

323. Foster, *Handbook to Life*, 192; Benson, *Birds and Beasts*, 118.

324. Peterson and Green, *Precolumbian Flora and Fauna*, 91.

325. Sahagún, *Florentine Codex*, 11:4.

326. Benson, *Birds and Beasts*, 44.

327. Sahagún, *Florentine Codex*, 11:54.

328. López Austin, *Cuerpo humano*, 1:419; Sahagún, *Florentine Codex*, vols. 4 and 5:42.

329. Schlesinger, *Animals and Plants of the Ancient Maya*, 183.

330. Peterson and Green, *Precolumbian Flora and Fauna*, 46; Schlesinger, *Animals and Plants of the Ancient Maya*, 183.

331. Milbrath, *Star Gods of the Maya*, 119.

332. Aguilar-Moreno, *Handbook to Life*, 178.

333. Peterson and Green, *Precolumbian Flora and Fauna*, 46; Benson, *Birds and Beasts*, 94–95.

334. Taube, *Major Gods of Ancient Yucatán*, 29, fig. h.

335. Carrasco, "Mask Flange," 19n9.

336. Benson, *Birds and Beasts*, 97; Scherer, *Mortuary Landscapes*, 63.

337. Foster, *Handbook to Life*, 186.

338. Benson, *Birds and Beasts*, 99; De Landa, *Yucatán Before and After*, 36.

339. Taube, *Major Gods of Ancient Yucatán*, 95, fig. e, 99.

340. Foster, *Handbook to Life*, 161; Milbrath, *Star Gods of the Maya*, 253.

341. Benson, *Birds and Beasts*, 87.

342. Schlesinger, *Animals and Plants of the Ancient Maya*, 187; Peterson and Green, *Precolumbian Flora and Fauna*, 20.

343. Peterson and Green, *Precolumbian Flora and Fauna*, 20; Benson, *Birds and Beasts*, 91–92.

344. Christenson, *Popol Vuh*, 84–88.

345. Durán, *Book of Gods*, 402.

346. Seler, Thompson, and Comparato, *Collected Works*, 247.

347. Sahagún, *Florentine Codex*, 11:30–31.

348. Sahagún, 11:13.

349. Christenson, *Popol Vuh*, 172.

350. Ortiz de Montellano, *Aztec Medicine*, 133.

351. López Austin, *Cuerpo humano*, 1:419; Sahagún, *Florentine Codex*, vols. 4 and 5:42.

352. Sahagún, *Primeros Memoriales*, 175.

353. Sahagún, *Florentine Codex*, 11:39.

354. Sahagún, 11:31.

355. Seler, Thompson, and Comparato, *Collected Works,* 194.

356. De la Serna, *Tratado De Las Idolatrías,* 198.

357. Milbrath, *Star Gods of the Maya,* 253.

358. Kettunen, "Nasal Motifs," 280n150.

359. Sahagún, *Florentine Codex,* 11:52.

360. Sahagún, 11:32.

Bibliography

Aguilar-Moreno, Manuel. *Handbook to Life in the Aztec World*. Oxford: Oxford University Press, 2006.

Aguilera, Carmen. "El Simbolismo del quetzal en mesoamerica." En *Animales y plantas en la cosmovisión mesoamericana,* coordinadora por Yolotl González Torres, 221–240. Mexico City: Sociedad Mexicana para el Estudio de las Religiones, 2001.

Álvarez Esteban, Manuel. "La entidada animica wahyis en el Clasico Tardío maya y su relación con el poder ritual," Academia (website) 2014–15, 5.

Ashmore, Wendy. "Deciphering Maya Architectural Plans." In *New Theories on the Ancient Maya,* edited by Elin C. Danien and Robert J. Sharer, 173–84. Philadelphia: University of Pennsylvania Press, 1992.

———. "Gender and Landscapes." In *Handbook of Gender in Archaeology,* edited by Sarah Milledge Nelson, 199–218. Lanham, Md.: AltaMira Press, 2006.

———. "Site-Planning Principles and Concepts of Directionality among the Ancient Maya." *Latin American Antiquity* 2, no. 3 (1991): 199–226.

Bell, Catherine. *Ritual: Perspectives and Dimensions.* New York: Oxford University Press, 1997.

Benson, Elizabeth P. *Birds and Beasts of Ancient Latin America.* Gainesville: University Press of Florida, 1997.

Bernatz, Michele M. "Redefining God L: The Spatial Realm of a Maya Earth Lord." In *Maya Imagery, Architecture, and Activity: Space and Spatial Analysis in Art History,* edited by Maline D. Werness-Rude and Kaylee R. Spencer, 140–77. Albuquerque: University of New Mexico Press, 2015.

Blainey, Marc G. "Techniques of Luminosity: Iron-Ore Mirrors and Entheogenic Shamanism among the Ancient Maya." In *Manufactured Light: Mirrors in the Mesoamerican Realm,* edited by Emiliano Gallaga and Marc G. Blainey, 179–206. Boulder: University Press of Colorado, 2016.

Boone, Elizabeth H. *Cycles of Time and Meaning in the Mexican Books of Fate.* Austin: University of Texas Press, 2007.

Brady, James E., and Wendy Ashmore. "Mountains, Caves, Water: Ideational Landscapes of the Ancient Maya." In *Archaeologies of Landscape: Contemporary Perspectives*, edited by Brady and Ashmore, 124–145. Malden, Mass.: Blackwell, 1999.

Buenaflor, Erika. *Cleansing Rites of Curanderismo: Limpias Espirituales of Ancient Mesoamerican Shamans*. Rochester, Vt.: Bear & Company, 2018.

———. *Curanderismo Soul Retrieval: Ancient Shamanic Wisdom to Restore the Sacred Energy of the Soul*. Rochester, Vt.: Bear & Company, 2019.

———. *Sacred Energies of the Sun and Moon: Shamanic Rites of Curanderismo*. Rochester, Vt.: Bear & Company, 2020.

Burdick, Catherine E. "Text and Image in Classic Maya Sculpture: A.D. 600–900." Master's thesis, University of Illinois at Chicago, 2010.

Burkhart, Louise M. "Flowery Heaven: The Aesthetic of Paradise in Nahuatl Devotional Literature." *RES: Anthropology and Aesthetics* 21 (Spring 1992): 88–109.

———. *The Slippery Earth: Nahua-Christian Moral Dialogue in Sixteenth-Century Mexico*. Tucson: University of Arizona Press, 1989.

Carrasco, David. *Quetzalcoatl and the Irony of Empire: Myths and Prophecies in the Aztec Tradition*. Chicago: University of Chicago Press, 1982.

Carrasco, Michael D. "Epilogue: Portals, Turtles, and Mythic Places," In *Maya Imagery, Architecture, and Activity,* edited by Maline D. Werness-Rude and Kaylee R. Spencer, 374–411. Albuquerque: University of New Mexico Press, 2015.

———. "The Mask Flange Iconographic Complex: The Art, Ritual, and History of a Maya Sacred Image." Ph.D. diss., University of Texas at Austin, August 2005.

Christenson, Allen J., ed. and trans. *Popol Vuh: Sacred Book of the Quiché Maya People*. Mesoweb (electronic publication), 2007.

Cogolludo, Diego López de. *Historia de Yucatán*. Campeche: Comisión de Historia, 1954.

Craine, Eugene R., and Reginald C. Reindorp. *The Codex Perez and the Book of Chilam Balam of Maní*. Norman: University of Oklahoma Press, 1979.

De la Garza, Mercedes. *Sueno y Extasis: Vision Chamanica de Los Nahuas y Los Mayas*. Mexico City: UNAM, 2012.

De Landa, Diego. *Yucatán Before and After the Conquest*. Translated by William Gates. New York: Dover, 1978.

De la Serna, Jacinto. *Tratado De Las Idolatrías Supersticiones, Hechicerias, y Otras Costumbres De Las Razas Aborigenes De Mexico*. Muntaner, Barcelona: Linkgua Ediciones S.L., 2008.

Durán, Diego. *The Book of Gods and Rites and the Ancient Calendar.* Translated by F. Horcasitas and Doris Heyden. Norman: University of Oklahoma Press, 1971.

Fernández, Adela. *Dioses prehispánicos de México: Mitos y deidades del panteón nahuatl.* Mexico City: Panorama Editorial, 2006.

Foster, Lynn V. *Handbook to Life in the Ancient Mayan World.* Oxford: Oxford University Press, 2002.

Freidel, David, Linda Schele, and Joy Parker. *Maya Cosmos: Three Thousand Years on the Shaman's Path.* New York: William Morrow, 1993.

Fridberg, Diana. "Peccaries in Ancient Maya Economy, Ideology, and Iconography." Master's thesis, Harvard University, March 2005.

Furst, Jill Leslie McKeever. *The Natural History of the Soul in Ancient Mexico.* New Haven, Conn.: Yale University Press, 1995.

Gossen, H. Gary. "Animal Souls, Coessences, and Human Destiny in Mesoamerica." In *Monsters, Tricksters, and Sacred Cows: Animal Tales and American Identities,* edited by A. James Arnold, 80–107. Charlottesville: University of Virginia Press, 1996.

Grofe, Michael J. *The Recipe for Rebirth: Cacao as Fish in the Mythology and Symbolism of the Ancient Maya.* Department of Native American Studies, University of California at Davis, September 23, 2007.

Grube, Nikolai, and Werner Nahm. "A Census of Xibalba: A Complete Inventory of Way Characters on Maya Ceramics." In *The Maya Vase Book: A Corpus of Rollout Photographs of Maya Vases,* vol. 4, edited by Barbara Kerr and Justin Kerr, 683–715. New York: Kerr Associates, 1994.

———. "A Sign for the Syllable mi." *Research Reports on Ancient Maya Writing* 33 (1990): 15–26.

Harner, Michael. *The Way of the Shaman.* San Francisco: HarperOne, 1990.

Hernández, Alfonso Arellano. "Llego el caimán: los dragones en el mundo maya." En *Animales y plantas en la cosmovisión mesoamericana,* coordinadora por Yolotl González Torres, 192–220. Mexico City: Sociedad Mexicana para el Estudio de las Religiones, 2001.

Hernández, Christine, and Victoria R. Bricker. "The Inauguration of Planting in the Borgia and Madrid Codices." In *The Madrid Codex: New Approaches to Understanding an Ancient Maya Manuscript,* edited by Gabrielle Vail and Anthony Aveni, 277–320. Boulder: University Press of Colorado, 2004.

Houston, Stephen D., *Hieroglyphs and History at Dos Pilas: Dynastic Politics of the Classic Maya.* Austin: University of Texas Press, 1993.

Houston, Stephen D., and David Stuart. "The Way Glyph: Evidence for 'Coessences' among the Classic Maya." In *The Decipherment of Ancient Maya Writing,* edited by Stephen Houston, Oswaldo Chinchilla Mazariegos, and David Stuart, 449–62. Norman: University of Oklahoma Press, 2001.

Houston, Stephen D., David Stuart, and Karl A. Taube. "Image and Text on the 'Jauncy Vase.'" In *The Maya Vase Book: A Corpus of Rollout Photographs of Maya Vases,* vol. 3, edited by Barbara Kerr and Justin Kerr, 504–523. New York: Kerr Associates, 1992.

———. *The Memory of Bones: Body, Being, and Experience among the Classic Maya.* Austin: University of Texas Press, 2011.

Hull, Kerry, Mark Wright, and Rob Fergus. "Avian Actors: Transformation, Sorcery, and Prognostication in Mesoamerica." In *Raptor and Human: Falconry and Bird Symbolism throughout the Millennia on a Global Scale,* edited by Karl-Heinz Gersmann and Oliver Grimm, 347–66. Kiel, Hamburg, Ger.: Murmann Publishers, 2018.

Ingalls, Victoria A. "The Quadripartite Badge: Narratives of Power and Resurrection in Maya Iconography," Master's thesis, Texas State University, 2009.

Kettunen, Harri. "Nasal Motifs in Maya Iconography." Master's thesis, Renvall Institute, University of Helsinki, August, 2006.

León-Portilla, Miguel. *Aztec Thought and Culture: A Study of the Ancient Nahuatl Mind.* Translated by Jack Emory Davis. Norman: University of Oklahoma Press, 1963.

León-Portilla, Miguel, Earl Shorris, Sylvia S. Shorris, Ascensión H. de León-Portilla, and Jorge Klor de Alva. *In the Language of Kings: An Anthology of Mesoamerican Literature, Pre-Columbian to the Present.* London: Norton, 2001.

Looper, Matthew G. "Women-Men (and Men-Women): Classic Maya Rulers and the Third Gender." In *Ancient Maya Women,* edited by Traci Arden, 171–202. Walnut Creek, Calif.: Altamira Press, 2002.

Lopes, Luís. *Some Notes on Fireflies.* Departamento de Ciência de Computadores (website).

López Austin, Alfredo. "Cuarenta clases de magos del mundo náhuatl." *Estudios de cultura Náhuatl* 7 (1967): 87–117.

———. *Cuerpo humano e ideología: Las concepciones de los antiguos nahuas.* 2 vols. Mexico City: Instituto de Investigaciones Antropológicas, 1984.

———. *Human Body and Ideology of the Ancient Nahuas.* Translated by Thelma Ortiz de Montellano and B. R. Ortiz de Montellano. 2 vols. Salt Lake City: University of Utah Press, 1988.

———. *The Myths of the Opossum: Pathways of Mesoamerican Mythology.* Translated by Bernard R. Ortiz de Montellano and Thelma Ortiz de Montellano. Albuquerque: University of New Mexico Press, 1993.

———. *Tamoanchan, Tlalocan: Places of Mist.* Translated by Bernard R. Ortiz de Montellano and Thelma Ortiz de Montellano. Niwot: University Press of Colorado, 1997.

Maffie, James. *Aztec Philosophy: Understanding a World in Motion.* Boulder: University Press of Colorado, 2014.

Martin, Simon, Kathleen Berrin, and Mary Miller. *Courtly Art of the Ancient Maya.* New York: Thames & Hudson, 2004.

Mazariegos, Oswaldo C. *Art and Myth of the Ancient Maya.* New Haven, Conn.: Yale University Press, 2017.

———. "Of Birds and Insects: The Hummingbird Myth in Ancient Mesoamerica." *Ancient Mesoamerica* 21 (2010): 45–61.

Mexicolore. "God of the Month: Tlaloc," Mexicolore (website).

Milbrath, Susan. "Gender Roles of Lunar Deities in Postclassic Central Mexico and Their Correlations with the Maya Area." *Estudios de Cultura Nahuatl* 25 (1995): 45–93.

———. "Seasonal Imagery in Ancient Mexican Almanacs of the Dresden Codex and Codex Borgia." In *Das Bild der Jahreszeiten im Wandel der Kulturen und Zeiten,* edited by Thierry Greub, 117–42. Munich: Wilhelm Fink Verlag, 2013.

———. *Star Gods of the Maya: Astronomy in Art, Folklore, and Calendars.* Austin: University of Texas Press, 1999.

———. "Xochiquetzal and the Lunar Cult of Central Mexico." In *Precious Greenstone, Precious Feather In Chalchihuitl in Quetzalli: Essays on Ancient Mexico in Honor of Doris Heyden,* edited by Elizabeth Quiñones Keber, 31–55. Lancaster City, Calilf.: Labyrinthos, 2000.

Molina, Fray Alonso de. *Vocabulario en Lengua Castellano y Mexicana.* Edited by Miguel León-Portilla. Facsimile edition. Mexico City: Editorial Porrúa, 1970.

Moreno, Daniel. "Los espiritus del sueno: wahyis y enfermedad entre los mayas del periodo Clásico." Master's thesis, Escuela Nacional de Antrpologia e Historia, 2011.

Nequatewa, Edmund. *Truth of a Hopi and Other Clan Stories of Shungopovi.* Flagstaff: Museum of Northern Arizona Bulletin No. 8, Northern Arizona Society of Science and Art, 1936.

Olivier, Guilhem. *Mockeries and Metamorphoses of an Aztec God: Tezcatlipoca, "Lord of the Smoking Mirror."* Boulder: University Press of Colorado, 2008.

Ortiz de Montellano, Bernard R. *Aztec Medicine, Health, and Nutrition.* New Brunswick, N.J.: Rutgers University Press, 1990.

Peterson, Jeanette F., and Judith S. Green. *Precolumbian Flora and Fauna: Continuity of Plant and Animal Themes in Mesoamerican Art.* San Diego, Calif.: Mingei International Museum of World, 1990.

Pineda, Gabriel E. "La fauna de Ehécatl." En *Animales y plantas en la cosmovisión mesoamericana,* coordinadora por Yolotl González Torres, 255–304. Mexico City: Sociedad Mexicana para el Estudio de las Religiones, 2001.

Proskouriakoff, Tatiana. "Portraits of Women in Maya Art." In *The Decipherment of Ancient Maya Writing,* edited by Stephen D. Houston, Oswaldo Chinchilla Mazariegos, and David Stuart, 312–67. Norman: University of Oklahoma Press, 2001.

Quenon, Michel, and Genevieve Le Fort, "Rebirth and Resurrection in Maize God Iconography," In *The Maya Vase Book: A Corpus of Rollout Photographs of Maya Vases,* vol. 5, edited by Barbara Kerr and Justin Kerr, 884–902. New York: Kerr Associates, 1997.

Roys, Ralph L., ed. and trans. *The Book of Chilam Balam of Chumayel.* 2nd ed. Norman: University of Oklahoma Press, 1967.

———. *Ritual of the Bacabs.* Norman: University of Oklahoma Press, 1965.

Ruiz de Alarcón, Hernando. *Aztec Sorcerers in Seventeenth Century Mexico: The Treatise on Superstitions by Hernando Ruiz de Alarcón.* Edited and translated by M. D. Coe and C. Whittaker. Albany: State University of New York Press, 1982.

Sahagún, Bernardino de. *Florentine Codex: General History of the Things of New Spain.* 2nd ed. Translated by Arthur J. O. Anderson and Charles E. Dibble. 12 vols. Santa Fe, N. Mex.: School of American Research and University of Utah, 2012.

———. *The Primeros Memoriales of Fray Bernardino de Sahagún.* Translated by Thelma D. Sullivan. Edited by H. B. Nicolson, Arthur J. O. Anderson, Charles E. Dibble, Eloise Quiñones Keber, and Wayne Ruwet. Norman: University of Oklahoma Press, 1997.

Saturno, William, Franco D. Rossi, David Stuart, and Heather Hurst. "A Maya Curia Regis: Evidence for a Hierarchical Specialist Order at Xultun, Guatemala." *Ancient Mesoamerica* 10 (2017): 1–18.

Schele, Linda, and Mary Miller. *The Blood of Kings: Dynasty and Ritual in Maya Art.* New York: George Braziller, Inc., 1986.

Scherer, Andrew K. *Mortuary Landscapes of the Classic Maya: Rituals of Body and Soul.* Austin: University of Texas Press, 2015.

Schlesinger, Victoria. *Animals and Plants of the Ancient Maya: A Guide.* Austin: University of Texas Press, 2001.

Seler, Eduard, J. Eric S. Thompson, and Frank E. Comparato. *Collected Works in Mesoamerican Linguistics and Archaeology.* 6 vols. Culver City, Calif.: Labyrinthos, 1996.

Stone, A. J. *Images from the Underworld: Naj Tunich and the Tradition of Maya Cave Painting.* Austin: University of Texas Press, 1995.

Stone, Andrea, and Marc Zender. *Reading Maya Art: A Hieroglyphic Guide to Ancient Maya Painting and Sculpture.* New York: Thames & Hudson, 2011.

Stuart, David. *The Inscriptions from Temple XIX at Palenque: A Commentary.* San Francisco: The Pre-Columbian Art Research Institute, 2005.

———. *The Order of Days: Unlocking the Secrets of the Ancient Maya.* New York: Three Rivers, 2011.

———. "The Way Beings." In *Glyphs on Pots: Decoding Classic Maya Ceramics.* Sourcebook for the 29th Maya Meetings at University of Texas at Austin, March 11–16, 2005.

Stuart, David, and George Stuart. *Palenque: Eternal City of the Maya.* New York: Thames & Hudson, 2008.

Taube, Karl A. "Ancient and Contemporary Maya Conceptions about the Field and Forest." In *The Lowland Maya Area: Three Millennia at the Human-Wildland Interface,* edited by Scott Fedick, Michael Allen, Juan Jiménez-Osornio, and A. Gómez-Pompa, 461–92. Binghamton, N.Y.: Food Products Press/Haworth Press, 2003.

———. "The Birth Vase: Natal Imagery in Ancient Maya Myth and Ritual." In *The Maya Vase Book: A Corpus of Rollout Photographs of Maya Vases,* vol. 4, edited by Barbara Kerr and Justin Kerr, 650–85. New York: Kerr Associates, 1994.

———. "At Dawn's Edge: Tulúm, Santa Rita, and Floral Symbolism in the International Style of Late Postclassic Mesoamerica." In *Astronomers, Scribes, and Priests: Intellectual Interchange between the Northern Maya Lowlands and Highland Mexico in the Late Postclassic Period,* edited by Gabrielle Vail and Christine Hernández, 145–91. Washington, D.C.: Dumbarton Oaks, 2010.

———. "Flower Mountain: Concepts of Life, Beauty, and Paradise among the Classic Maya." *RES: Anthropology and Aesthetics* 45 (Spring 2004): 69–98.

———. *The Legendary Past: Aztec and Maya Myths.* Austin: University of Texas Press, 1993.

———. *The Major Gods of Ancient Yucatán: Studies in Pre-Columbian Art and Archaeology,* no. 32. Washington, D.C.: Dumbarton Oaks, 1992.

———. "Maws of Heaven and Hell: The Symbolism of the Centipede and Serpent in Classic Maya Religion." In *Antropologia de la eternidad: La Muerte en la cultura maya,* edited by Andrés Ciudad Ruiz, Maria Humberto Ruz Sosa, and María Josefa Iglesias Ponce de León, 404–42. Madrid: Sociedad de Española de Estudios Vayas, 2003.

———. *Olmec Art at Dumbarton Oaks.* Washington, D.C.: Dumbarton Oaks Research Library and Collection, 2004.

———. "The Symbolism of Jade in Classic Maya Religion." *Ancient Mesoamerica* 16, no. 1 (January 2005): 23–50.

———. "The Temple of Quetzalcoatl and the Cult of Sacred War at Teotihuacan." *Res: Anthropology and Aesthetics* 21 (1992): 53–87. Cambridge, Mass.: The Peabody Museum of Archaeology and Ethnology, Harvard University.

———. "The Turquoise Hearth: Fire, Self-Sacrifice, and the Central Mexican Cult of War." In *Mesoamerica's Classic Heritage: From Teotihuacan to the Aztecs,* edited by Davíd Carrasco, Lindsay Jones, and Scott Sessions, 269–340. Boulder: University Press of Colorado, 2000.

Taube, Karl A., William A. Saturno, David Stuart, and Heather Hurst. "The Murals of San Bartolo, El Petén, Guatemala Part 2: The West Wall." *Ancient America,* no. 10. The Boundary End Archaeology Research Center, 2010.

Taylor, Dicey. "Painted Ladies: Costumes for Women on Tepeu Ceramics." In *The Maya Vase Book: A Corpus of Rollout Photographs of Maya Vases,* vol. 3, edited by Barbara Kerr and Justin Kerr, 513–25. New York: Kerr Associates, 1992.

Tedlock, Dennis, ed. and trans. *Popol Vuh.* New York: Simon and Schuster, 1985.

———. *Popol Vuh: The Definitive Edition of the Mayan Book of the Dawn of Life and the Glories of Gods and Kings.* 2nd ed. New York: Touchstone, 1996.

Thompson, J. Eric S. *Maya Hieroglyphic Writing: An Introduction.* Norman: University of Oklahoma Press, 1960.

———. *Maya History and Religion.* Norman: University of Oklahoma Press, 1990.

Torres, González Yolotl. "Estudios de cultura Náhuatl." En *Animales y plantas en la cosmovisión mesoamericana,* coordinadora por Yolotl González Torres, 375–89. Mexico City: Sociedad Mexicana para el Estudio de las Religiones, 2001.

Turner, Andrew. "Cultures at the Crossroads: Art, Religion, and Interregional Interaction in Central Mexico, AD 600–900." Ph.D. diss., Department of Anthropology, University of California at Riverside, March 2016.

Velásquez García, Erik. "The Maya Flood Myth and the Decapitation of the Cosmic Caiman." *The PARI Journal* 7, no. 1 (2006): 1–10.

———. "Nuevas ideas en torno a los espiritus wahyis pintados en las vasijas maya: hechicería, enfermedades y banquetes oníricos en el arte prehispánico." In *XXXIII Coloquio internacional de historia del arte: Estética del mal conceptos y representaciones,* edited by Erik Velásquez García, 561–85. Mexico City: UNAM, 2013.

———. "Reflections on the Codex Style and the Princeton Vessel." *The PARI Journal* 10, no. 1 (2009): 1–16.

Werness-Rude, Maline D., and Kaylee R. Spencer, eds. *Maya Imagery, Architecture, and Activity: Space and Spatial Analysis in Art History.* Albuquerque: University of New Mexico Press, 2015.

Zender, Marc. "On the Morphology of Intimate Possession in Maya Languages and Classic Mayan Glyphic Nouns." In *The Linguistics of Maya Writing.* Edited by Soren Wichmann, 195–209. Salt Lake City: The University of Utah Press, 2004.

———. "A Study of Classic Maya Priesthood." Master's thesis, University of Calgary, July 2004.

Zralka, Jarosław, Christophe Helmke, Laura Sotelo, and Wiesław Koszkul. "The Discovery of a Beehive and the Identification of Apiaries among the Ancient Maya," *Latin American Antiquity* 29, no. 3 (2018): 514–31.

Index

Numbers in *italics* preceded by *pl.* refer to color insert plate numbers.

196